I Don't Think You Understand What I Mean

By

Ralph H Weaver

Edited by

Joan E Savage

Cover Illustration by Dan Savage

Other Books written by Ralph H. Weaver
Imagining the Works of the Divine - seeking the
works of the Divine in our relationships with others.

Coming Soon -
On the Edge of the Black Hole - a tale of Mr.
Weaver's battle with Alzheimer's Disorder.

Books are available in both digital and print editions

CONTENTS

I Don't Think You Understand What I Mean

Acknowledgments

I wish to acknowledge the different types of individuals who, with great patience, endured my inquiries and did not hesitate to wander with me through the different entanglements of logic I have written in this book.

My wife and I pay tribute to the different professions and the persons that were really good at what they do: the doctors, lawyers, accountants, mechanics and others like those at Goss Rental Equipment, who without their efforts and patience we would have not survived. We do not take their efforts casually.

More than anything else there are the students, especially the young ladies who while teaching Mathematics would make an inquiry about some problem and patiently wait until I could find the answers. To the Emilys, Karens, Cindys, Joans and Julies of the world, I raise my highest gratitude.

Forward

Through the years, I have enjoyed many conversations with a variety of people I have visited in bus stations, laundromats, garages, work places and in a variety of different waiting rooms. Invariably, the conversation seems to get around to opinions, beliefs, theories and what have you. So many times I have had the person engaged in the conversation say to me, "You should write this stuff down, I would like to read it" or "That's good stuff, you have helped me." Of course, I have paid little attention to such statements and consigned the compliments to politeness. Friends I have talked to have asked the same thing. Lately, my wife of many years has belabored me into writing my story. As time goes by, I run again and again into individuals who say, "When are you going to write those ideas down?", "Give us the history of your life, the how and why of your thought life, and the ideas that have helped us along the way." So, as I approach 80 years of age, and because of the insistence of people I love, I will attempt. The purpose of doing this project is found in the first chapter of Luke's book. Luke wrote those things down so that we may know and receive help in our faith. So, I write that you too might receive some boost in your journey from a modern day pilgrim. I hope that it will help and encourage you.

As of late when I talk to persons my age and they begin to tell their stories, I have been shocked at how almost identical their story is to mine. I have met and talked to many of these folks while they were engaged in volunteer work. Their journey is our journey, and their story is our story. Even today, I have conversations with younger people and they seem to have the same story. We do not write this for everyone, but for those who have experienced some rough patches and are in need of a little reassurance.

Now, to those of you who now have positioned yourselves, as it says in Psalm 1:1, in the seat of the scornful I suggest you take your spiritual tutus and dance somewhere else.

Chapter 1
Environment of Life

We begin with Isaiah 1:18 (KJV). "Come now, and let us reason together, saith the LORD: though your sins be as scarlet, they shall be as white as snow; though they be red like crimson, they shall be as wool."

This remarkable statement written so many years ago in antiquity has the writer appeal to us asking us to consider the process of reasoning. The projected thought in question is not whimsical, but the writer states that through the reasoning process, which involves a cognitive relationship with our Heavenly Father, we will become pure. We can alter our acceptance by others, persons in our environment, by having an essence of purity. This essence of purity will make us easier to talk with, because humans do not like to deal with dirt. So, if we can manage a better appearance through reasoning, then our neighbor feels like he is getting the best treatment possible out of us.

I am writing this in the hope that the story may be of use to someone in their journey of life. My mother had a saying that she constantly used: "It's a poor bird that bedaddles in its own nest." With that in mind, and to honor her wishes, the background for my family life will have to be sugar-coated. I mean really sugar coated. I will attempt to show those things which influenced my state of mind and leave out anything that would bring dishonor to her. She was a victim, living among a tribe of uncaring, cruel people who were always talking about how much they loved one another. Well, let me say my earliest comment on the subject of love: If it smells like hate, tastes like hate, and feels like hate, brothers and sisters, its hate.

To do the work that I wish to do, you may perhaps bear with me. My intention is to first relate my life and the many turns it took. I would not embellish or distort life. I am fully conscience of the concept that any grain of untruth that is written here will diminish the effect of providing those words that will enhance, and not detract, from the reader's understanding. I really would like to reveal to the reader life as it happened, and how I arrived at a badly disturbed mind. This is to offer a kind of primer on how, through reason and acceptance of help from others, I was able to reach a state of real contentment. The primer will be good for other rascals like me, and if you are one, enable you to move forward in life.

As I have stated in the forward, for many years I have felt that my life was unique and I was the only one to have to deal with the trials that life had to offer. The following entry revealed the discovery that I am not unique. There is a story that I used to tell about my experience working on the dam at St. Croix Falls, Wisconsin. The surface of the dam had become rotten and a company was hired to replace the concrete surface. I was serving as a pastor of a small church at the time and desperate for funds, so I hired on.

You would take a fifty pound jack-hammer with a two foot drill bit; belly high you went across the bottom of the dam drilling holes. You would shove a galvanized pipe in the holes, throw planks on the pipes, and stepped up to the next level. There were no guard rails, just empty air behind you. Standing on the two–by-twelve planks placed on the pipes, you worked across the dam, belly high at a time and up the side of dam you went, this made a type of scaffolding on the face of the dam. You were warned that you must pay attention as you could get the drill stuck in the dam, and if that happened you had to get it out yourself. Well!!, I did just that. So, here I was about thirty feet up yanking on the drill, no guard rail if you please, and all of a sudden the drill let loose and I thought I was a goner. I looked around to see if the boss had seen me, for you would be fired if you stuck the drill due to failure to pay attention and I needed the money. Once you reached the top, you took a ninety pound air hammer and began chipping the rotten concrete away. I will not bore you with that aspect, but that was even scarier.

The funny thing about me is that even after fifteen years of climbing ladders, falling, and what have you, I began to be really afraid of heights when there were no guard rails.

To make a long story short, I quit telling the story for no one would believe it anyway. The point is that at 79 years of age, I did start to tell the story to an older gentleman. I nearly fell off my chair, because before I got part way through the story, he interrupted me. He said I know what you are talking about and he related how he, when younger took a … Wow! No sarcastic look from him; no disbelief from him. Yes, the story is not unique, we, both, did do these things and we did survive and we did use the Good Book to strengthen and straighten us out. Yea, yea, yea, the same story. Just two old believers regaling each other with life and faith and the instrument, the Good Book, that saw us through.

My father was born in 1891, and my mother was born in 1894, so the family tells me. There seems to be some disagreement on this information, but my wife placed in our book of records these dates. The data was supplied by my mother to my wife and I am inclined to believe her. My great-grandfather lost his health following Sherman through the swamps of the Carolinas. The information is only important in that it relates some of my heritage. My father went through the fourth grade by the time he was twelve, and when he married my mother he still could not read. When he was young, he was farmed out to other farmers, as was the custom, and the money was used by the family to survive. This explains why he took so long in a one room school house to reach the fourth grade. When you worked for farmers, you did not go year-round to school, but only as the time allowed. My mother told me that she taught my father to read, and though others in the family may disagree with the information; I am inclined to take her word for it as well.

The point of this is to show that they were poor, life was rough, and this affected the way I was raised. It was a rough no-holds-barred existence. I don't recall a paddling as such, but if you got your mother's attention, her solution was to beat you with whatever was handy: hoe handles, boards, what have you. My father never paddled me either. He, with a grin on his face and no sign of anger, simply hit you in the head with his fist. This engendered a certain level of fear and you did not offend very often. You might conclude that we developed a hatred for these folks, but actually just the opposite was the result. You had a very high level of respect for these people. You hear people say there was a lot of love in our family, but this word caused me no end of confusion. But more about the word "love" and why it causes so much confusion later in the book.

My mother inherited a nice sum of money, and she told me that her intention had been to buy three houses that she knew of and pay for them in cash. The family would live in one house and she would rent the other two, and she would then have some security in her family's life. My father and grandfather wanted to buy a large farm, and, unbeknownst to her, took the money and paid the down payment on a farm belonging to one of mother's relatives. There was a balance owed, and they were supposed to pay the balance off as crops came to maturity. My grandfather, John Paul, said he would pay the money to the aunt; he would have all the money come to him and then he would make the payment.

Through friends in the community, who knew him well, I heard about his reputation. He was the talk of many families. They said he was a person who liked to ride in his Model T Ford and make a big show. What he did was spend the money on carousing and never paid the aunt. When the day of reckoning came, we were thrown out on the street. My mother lost it and could not be consoled. This happened, of course, before I was born and I have my mother's word for it.

I never saw my grandfather in our home until he was ready to die and Mom allowed him to live there for a few days until his death. He was a big man, and I remember even in his old age he could sit the four youngest on his knees with plenty of room. I remember that experience; he was to us a giant.

My sister, Bernice, said they moved the family into an old barn and hung sheets up for walls and lived that way. My father then received an acre of ground as part of an inheritance and built a fine home on it. In that home, in the front room, I was born. The year was 1931 and my younger sister was born shortly after making 10 children in all. Dad owed about seven hundred dollars on the place and was worried about losing it. He met a fellow who bragged that his home was free and clear, and he was willing to trade Dad his property for ours and assume our debt. Dad, without checking things out, made the trade. It turns out the man was losing the property; it was about to be foreclosed on. Dad moved the family in, the bank foreclosed on it, and, you guessed it, back into a shed again.

The family found a hundred acre plus farm that a man named Shank was willing to rent on shares. We moved onto the farm, and there we lived until I was about 9 years of age. I am unclear of exactly how old I was when we moved from the farm, but my age estimation is close. While on the farm, the oldest sister was married and left. My oldest brother was married and he left. My two older sisters moved out and went to work for a woman in a neighboring town who owned a restaurant of sorts. My two sisters lived above the establishment and waited tables.

There were six remaining: four boys and two girls. Mr. Shank, the landlord, was referred to as "old man Shank." Mr. Shank offered my dad the farm based on a corn dollar. Corn prices fluctuated from year to year, and an acre, on average, could produce so many bushels of corn per year. Dad could farm the land and pay him at harvest time a percentage of the produce. It may have been fifty-fifty or some other agreed amount. I understood from my mother that the sum owed amounted to about three to five thousand dollars. It was years later I learned that the farm was sold in the eighties for about a half-million dollars. Wow, six strong boys and girls to work the farm, and according to Shank, Dad had plenty of free labor to farm the land. Dad had found carpentry work, and could continue to work his trade, but Dad turned him down. I asked Dad years later why. He replied, "I was not prepared to take another risk and fail."

The farm was sold out from under us, and, once more, you guessed it, back to living in a barn shed. We then moved into a tobacco strip house. Let me explain this to you. One of my fondest memories was concerning the growing and harvesting of tobacco. You planted tobacco in a hot bed and then later you took a tobacco planter and planted the plants in the ground. I was too young to help with that aspect, but I saw and I remembered it. As the tobacco grew, Dad would have the smaller children go row by row through the fields. He would pay a penny for every one hundred worms in a jar, for you got a better price if there were no holes in the leaf, and the tobacco worms were very hungry. I never got a penny, maybe one of the others did, but it was difficult to find one hundred worms and the things wouldn't keep, so you could not cheat.

In the fall when the frost had come and the tobacco was ready, you had tobacco laths and a sharp wedge-shaped metal thing that just fit the lath. You would bring the stalks in and sew them on a lath, and then hang them row on row in the barn. In January, on a cold freezing predawn morning, you would start a fire in the tight little strip house, bring the laths in and strip the leaves into a large box. Some men would come and look at the leaves and then make an offer for the crop. I tell this to you so you would know what a strip house shed was like. It was a tight little building with glazed windows. We moved in and mom hung blankets and sheets for rooms. There was mom, dad and six children. There were four boys and two girls. My grandmother owned the acre, and. for the first time, I met my father's mother. We had never visited her during my childhood, as she and the family had some kind of misunderstanding. At least that is what my grandmother inferred.

An agreement was made with grandmother, and permission granted to take down the barn and build a home out of it. Dad did this and my job was to take an anvil and a hammer and straighten out the salvaged nails. I spent hours doing that very same thing. When the building was up, with no indoor plumbing and no electricity, we moved in. There was no dry wall, and you could look through the boards and see the outside. There was no glass in the windows, but muslin cloth was tacked up to ensure no outsider could peer in. There was no stairs to the second floor bedrooms, but instead we used a ladder made of two by fours. I well remember Mom and Dad getting into a verbal argument on building a stair. Dad said its Sunday, and Mom spoke of an ox, and he built the stair under protest praying that his God would not hold it against him for working on Sunday. Working on Sunday was frowned upon whether you were church goers or not.

As he was paid each week, he bought windows, tar paper on the outside to hold out wind and rain and other things that made a livable house possible. Needless to say, we were always broke as no money could be spared for under garments and et cetera. Kids in schools scorned me, and I was regarded as white trash and I agreed with them. The stench of poverty hung in my nostrils for a long time. Finally the house was livable. It had electricity in it in the form of lights, and that was it as far as conveniences were concerned.

Then my grandmother died. My uncle had refused my grandmother's wish to give Dad title to the acre, and he sold the two houses for three thousand dollars. Once more we were out on the street. Dad got a plot of ground in Beavertown, Ohio that was attached to the old town dump. He made a cement basement house and we moved in. Now a basement home with a flat roof is prone to leaks and can be incredibly cold. It did leak, and it was cold. It had no shower or bath, but it did have an indoor toilet. Now, that is a convenience little appreciated. That, to me, was a fantastic improvement.

Here would be a good time to explain that aspect. We used what we called an old grey owl in the old house. This was used at night for toiletry. If a boy used the owl, it would be his job to carry it out in the morning, and it tended to be full. I determined that there was no way I was going to get that job, and, no matter how cold or dark the night, I used the outhouse. My dad would grunt with disgust when he awoke in the morning and saw barefoot-tracks in the snow, to the outhouse and back. He knew it was me; only someone stupid would do that. What no one knew was I had the habit of sneaking matches out, tearing pages from the catalogue, lighting the pages, and throwing it down the hole. I always had a warm seat in the winter. Once when dad arose too early, he saw the smoke and I was in trouble. I had to tell him what I was doing. He really got excited, and remarked that it was a wonder I did not blow the thing up as the gas from the deposit was capable of burning. He warned me that he did not want to catch me again. I said to myself you will not catch me as I was going to be more careful. I continued to do it. I felt a burnt backside was better than carrying out the owl. So, you see the indoor toilet facility is a wondrous invention.

This would be a good time to continue to cheer you up. When I was seven years old, my oldest brother was married. When I was getting ready to go to school in the fall, I had no school clothes. My oldest brother was a big fellow with about a 33 inch waist. My mother simply lopped the trousers off at the knees and told me to wear them. Here I was a skinny kid with skinny legs wearing short pants with great tubes of fabric for legs. The belt came with it. I punched a hole in the belt and gathered the trousers up at the waist and looped the belt through. The end of the belt extended around to somewhere in the back. When I began mowing yards and doing jobs for neighbors, I bought long pants and vowed to never wear short pants, and to this day I never have.

My next older sister would get a new pair of black belted shoes to start school with, and I was made to wear her old shoes. What a sight that must have been. One year I decided that I would no longer wear girl's shoes and a commotion commenced. My sister Bernice was working and owned a Ford; she decided to buy me a pair of shoes. She took me in her car into Dayton, Ohio off of Third Street and we went into the store and sat down. I had never had a pair of new shoes that I can recall, at least up to that time. I was excited and remember the whole incident in great detail. Bernice said take off the shoe I was wearing, and I did. Out came a foot with five toes sticking out from the sock. Around each toe nail was a black ring. Bernice gave a little cry, hit me with her elbow, and said put that shoe back on and takes off the other. Well out came the twin. She hit me with her elbow again, made me put the shoe back on, grabbed me by the wrist and out of the store we went flying. We went to another store, bought a pair of socks, then returned and I had new shoes.

I took my first bath in a tub when I was 16 and felt whoever invented the thing was divine. When younger, the family would take a wash tub in the kitchen, fill it with water, and give baths. My sisters went first, then my brothers and I was last. My brother Ken always got out of the tub with a grin. He let slip one time why he was grinning and from that time on you could not get me in the tub. If you tried, there would be a lot of mopping to do and it was not worth the effort. Well, enough of the levity. A little fun now and again is good. What is funny about these little stories is I felt deprived. I have since learned that I was not. Even today in America there are families living as we did. I have met them. They do the best they know how. They are also very good people, so you see this is more than just my story.

Dad slowly added to the home and finally a shell of a Cape Cod style house was added. My oldest brother somehow had figured out how to get title to the place and threw us out. Dad had a soft spot for him and the oldest brother could do no wrong. Dad built a cement house, and, while there, I left home. While I was away, my brother threw Mom and Dad out and they moved into a small rental apartment. It was in this apartment my mother passed away and finally found a home no one could move her out of.

It is my hope that you have stayed with me. I wanted you to see the environment I grew up in. In order to understand the story I had to tell how my life led from ignorance, hate and confusion to a way of thinking that brought about great joy, and anyone can participate in the process. Above all, you will see my coming to Christ was something that happened to me in spite of my distaste for a thing called Christianity. It was not an intellectual decision; my intellect abhorred this distasteful thing called Christianity.

Chapter 2
Reaction and Survival

I intend to not dwell on anything that does not show how I came to a certain mind set. I would like the reader to see how a person can overcome his anguish. Many times when I have been asked to write this, the person asking said please write and put me in the book. It is a story that belongs to many of us and I will try to tell it, but I have declined placing their names in the book, in my heart they are there.

My first recollection of my mother was on the Shank farm. I was about five years old. A young lady that my oldest brother brought to the home was standing in the kitchen with my mother. I had four older sisters and they were married or in school. At this young age, I was unaware of the differences between girls and boys, and I didn't care. But to me, there was something different about this young lady and I said to her, "How come you are so fat up on top." Wow! My mother's hand flew and hit me upside of the head. My ear hurt for a long time with a very sharp pain.

This then became the pattern of early youth. A slap in the head, a stick across the back, or one of my brothers whopping me for some crime known only to them. I honestly could not figure out what I was doing wrong. In school the same pattern persisted. I was five years old when school started and my birthday is in December. I graduated high school at

17 years of age, so you can figure it out. I was undersized at the time and was referred to as a runt, and the runt's lights did not appear to be on. Naturally, since this was when it was considered a rite of passage to find some runt and kick the bejabbers out of him. I fell prey to a variety of abuse, they would either say some nasty thing to me, or trip me, or whatever would come to mind. It seemed to me some teachers thought it hilarious to see a kid knocked across the gravel, ouch!

ONE favorite thing that a boy, who obviously had spent too much time in some of the same grade levels and so was a little larger than the rest of us, liked to do, is grab the fly of my pants and rip it open. He apparently liked to see buttons fly. I would go home and receive some discipline for not taking care of my pants and since it involved the fly area, I would hear some statements about the dangers of playing in areas that I shouldn't. I felt I had heard too many lectures on the subject, but it did make me wonder what I was missing. The boy persisted to do this until the eighth grade, when his father thought he would be better off behind a mule and a plow.

Thank the powers that be for drop-outs. I came to school in the ninth grade looking for the ones who had tormented me. I had by this time had a few scuffles and had come out really well for I had grown quite a lot. I wanted a piece of the idiots. Who cared if I got kicked out of school? When I looked around in the ninth grade for my tormentors, they were gone. When I asked about them, I was informed that they had quit school. Wow!! What a wonderful thing it was to have a system that eliminated that kind of, "I won't use the names that I was calling them at that time" person. I later worked as an educator and realized that my attitude was wrong, but freedom from bullies is a remarkable thing.

Yes, I learned very quickly. The rules were, keep your mouth shut, play the part of an idiot, and always remember the white gods over you, love for you to bow and show them the respect they think is due them. Here are some examples. In music class we had a teacher who apparently liked too much fried chicken. He was of the large economy type and he always carried a big book. I loved to give my rendition of singing, so I would hold forth with my idea of joyous singing. Suddenly he hit me on the top of the head with the book. This explained the book. The third time this happened I learned to not make any noise but softly pantomimed. You could get hit for not making any noise also, so you had to be an artist at the game.

I have been slapped in the face with the open hand, hit with rulers across the hand, made to stand in the corner with a funny hat, made to put my head down on the desk, and I spent a lot of time standing out of the room in the hall. We had a truly remarkable principal who roamed the halls and took those students to the office, where they met the board. He would come by, talk to me, ask how I was doing, and then one time he asked me a question. Would you like to work for a free lunch? He gave me a job in the cafeteria. I don't recall standing out in the hall after that. Who says that that there is no justice? A teacher named Miss Marker taught me to read and I went full force into reading. I read everything, lusty or not. I read biographies and autobiographies. I became lost in a world of words. I would take a book home at night, stay out of everyone's way and read.

One day we were walking to gym class, single file of course, and I had just been reading a book that today we would call undesirable. I was all smiles enjoying what I had read and musing over the story, asleep to my surroundings. The gym draft dodger teacher from World War II was leading and talking. All of a sudden I felt a hand around my throat, my feet off the floor, and my head banging against a locker and heard him say; "Don't you dare smirk when I am talking. For one week you will set in the bleachers and not be a part of the class." His favorite gym class was dodge ball. I never saw such an evil game in my life. We had a stout fellow who had spent too many years in the fourth, fifth and sixth grade. He had a remarkable arm and delighted with great accuracy to hit you in the head with the ball. I sat and watched the play and thought, "I wish I could remember the smirk on my face, I would patent it." After a week the instructor thought I had learned something, and indeed I had. I would stand in front of the weakest kid I could find when playing dodge ball, pretend to dodge, get hit and sit down. He would say, "Weaver you are the most uncoordinated idiot I have ever seen." Well, lockers and choke-holds may hurt my bones, but words would never hurt me.

You might cringe at the idea of me being called an idiot, but seventy years ago, "moron", "imbecile" and "stupid" were common stock, in addition to standing in the corner with a funny shaped hat on your head. The average sixteen-year-old drop-out was a genius at a repertoire of odd cruel phrases that make today's kids seem amateurs.

We had a superintendent that made all the poor kids sit in a darker corner of the cafeteria. One of us would sneak over and take mustard and catsup off one of the tables. The superintendent kept a sharp eye and would grab the condiments from us and say sack lunches did not pay for these things and he would berate us. When he retired, a wonderful man took his place. He let us have the condiments. I tell you nothing was more wonderful then to place catsup and mustard on a piece of bread, when the slice of bread is all you have to eat. His name was Adam Becker and I will never forget him. Adam Becker was the person who took care of me and gave me the cafeteria job. I loved him and all my life I have thought about him.

In the eighth grade we took an IQ test. Mr. Becker came into the room and said the highest IQ that he had found in school records belonged to two people. One was a girl named Arlene. He said Ralph was the other. I'm sure that the record did not stand very long. He said he wanted to challenge me to do better. Right out loud in front of the whole class he made those statements.

Wow, in the ninth grade things looked up, and I decided to try. I took Algebra and Latin, among other courses. The wonderful Algebra teacher saw my struggles and said if I would stay after school she would work with me. I did stay that day. I had a sister who was several years ahead of me in school. She was a very pretty girl, a sort of Shirley Temple type, she was full of mischief and loved to cause a little heat for others, she was always sorry when it went too far but still enjoyed a little stir. Come now, see the humor in this for I do and I wouldn't have missed any of it. She told Mom I was bad and had to stay after school for discipline. Well, all help broke loose. My mom went to school and confronted the principle who knew nothing about it. When he did not give a reason for the supposed discipline, with loud noise she found me and yanked me home. I can tell you my interest in learning stopped right there. Who wants that kind of trouble?

My father did not like teachers anyway. He said politicians and teachers were parasites living on the public dole. He said these folks don't use boards and steel to make something useful. These folks instead sit around and watch the mechanics of the world creating. My father said the people living on the public dole sit around like vultures waiting for some person to develop an idea and then tax the best of the man's labor. He said for me to read the story of "The Little Red Hen" and then I would understand. My father, who only went to the fourth grade, said every time a person on the public dole received a dollar, somewhere some entrepreneur invested ten dollars and before he could benefit from his efforts he had to pay the lazy public service first. Anything left over was the man's. When a good person makes something useful, they tax it and give the increase of a man's labor to teachers, whose main goal was to harass the ignorant, later I became a teacher. Now admit it, there is "hummer" in this.

My grandmother died and my uncle got a hold of the property and evicted us in the street. Cement basement house, here we come. I was made to live with my grandmother for three years previous to her passing. I never knew why my parents did not want me in the home, but I was happy and it was liberating. My grandmother was a wonderful Irish lady, so she said, and we got along great. She was my grandmother and I was her grandson. What a fine time I had and no way would she have kicked us out in the street upon her death. The place was sold for three or four thousand dollars.

My brother Ken liked to point out how dumb I was. He would say, "You don't know your rear end from a hole in the ground." Of course, I would deny the accuracy of his statement. He would take a stick and make two holes in the dirt. He would say, "This hole is your hind end and this one is a hole in the ground. Which one is the hole in the ground?" Of course, I would pick the one he said was my hind end. He would laugh and say, "See I told you. You don't know. They are both holes in the ground." He must have done that a dozen times, and I would always pick the wrong one. He enjoyed it immensely and so did I. It is better to be dumb and ignorant if you are too small to defend yourself. He was convinced I was stupid and I was convinced that he was dumber. I was raised with a bunch of people who thought nothing at all of going through my things. I grew up with it. I was the kid that worked mowing yards and so on. If Ken was short of money, he simply helped himself to mine. If he saw me with some money, he would say it was his and helped himself. No parent would ever come to my aid, after all, was not I an idiot.

At the end of the ninth grade, we moved into the cement block house and with the old attitude and mind-set, I entered the new school. I would not take it anymore. I was now starting to grow and was whip-cord hard. I thought a couple of kids were starting to pick on me and in class I walked up to one and hit him in the jaw with my fist. I walked over to the other and the instructor stopped me. "Relax those fists", he said. He went on about how I could not have been more wrong, these persons were just trying to be friendly and they did not even hold a grudge, in fact one of them invited me to swim in his swimming pool. I thought, how stupid can you get? The school was Fairmont High and the rest of the time I spent in school was uneventful. I graduated at the bottom of my class. I should say fifth from the bottom out of a class of 156. When I graduated from high school, the high school yearbook prophecy, which I still have, predicted that I would be living in the Beavertown dump, looking through trash for a living.

In the new school, in the new town, I was cut off from my resources for making money. For a long time I had taken care of myself. I ate in the school cafeteria in the old school and got a job working in the cafeteria in the new school. Eating in these school cafeterias allowed me, for the first time, to have food I could eat. Cafeteria food was wonderful and the cooks took good care of me. But I had no way of generating funds. One of the friends in the new school told me about a person who might give me work. He had a rep for helping young guys out. My friend told me which school bus to take. Back then you got on any school bus you wanted. In that age of innocence there was not that much trouble. I hopped on the bus and got off at a grocery store in what was called Far Hills. I was fourteen and without a work permit.

The man's name was Al Fabric. He talked to me and put me to work. What a fantastic person. When I got off work, I ran home on the railroad track. I would go to school, take the bus, worked until the store closed and then helped clean up, arriving at home about ten o'clock. I did not ask permission from any one. I lived with my grandmother for some years and this may have resulted in lulling the parents to not notice if I were home or not.

Think about it. Go to school, take the bus to work, arrive home late at night and not a single soul asked about my whereabouts. I had siblings living in the home, that years later were surprised to find out that I was working after school. How fortunate I was, money in my pocket and no one to answer to. After several weeks, Al said, "Be at the store at 4, in the morning, on Saturday." I got up at 3, ran to the store and Al took me to the market to buy produce. He would pick out what he wanted and I would take them to the truck. Then wonders of wonders, he would take me to a diner and buy me breakfast. It was the first time I had eaten in a restaurant. He would let me buy what I wanted and I ate while he sat and drank coffee. Think about it, working from four in the morning on Saturday until closing time at nine. I worked in the produce department which required tearing down the shelves, washing everything up and after about ten, I could go home. What a wonderful time I was having. Money in my pocket to buy food, clothing and whatever else I felt I needed.

Al had a rep for helping kids like me out and so the inspectors watched him carefully. I had no work permit and he would say go to the bathroom, lock the door and stay until I come for you. The inspector would talk to the young persons on staff, checking for work permits and leave. Suddenly there would be a banging on the door, "Weaver, get your (blank) rear end out here, I never saw such a lazy rear end." And I would follow him like a puppy dog, happy in my new found environment.

I was a White Anglo-Saxon Protestant and familiar with "Fox's Book of Martyrs." I had heard how bad the Catholics were and here was this wonderful Roman Catholic treating me better than any Protestant Christian I had ever met. Let's say I had doubts about what I had been taught. Later in life, I lived in Minnesota and a Jewish business man befriended me. Gave me a job and Sonny Swartz was everything I expected a man to be. Yes, I had doubts about some of what I had been taught in the home.

I graduated as I said at the bottom of my class. I got a job working for Frigidaire at Moraine Products and in 1950; I made 100 dollars a week take-home pay. I later learned that a school superintendant made only fifteen hundred a year. What a life. Money to burn, slot machines to play and trouble to get into. My two older brothers had started college with intent to be preachers. They had undergone a remarkable change and were attempting to steer me in that direction. Ken said that the way I was going, I would get myself killed and that would cause undue hardship on the family as finances were bad and it would cost money to bury.

One Sunday night, my brother, Harry asked me to go to church with him. I loved to sing "The Whiffenpoof Song" in front of him, especially the line, "doomed from here to eternity." Wow, that brought some contortions on his face. He looked like he was going to explode and I was delighted. Remember, his new faith held that he had to have understanding and no beatings were allowed. Finally I agreed to go with him. We arrived late and the altar call was being given. They were singing the hymn "Just as I Am" and the lyrics tell how God will accept you, regardless of your sins. "Don't worry", the preacher said, "God's job is to clean you up. Just relax and the Lord will do the rest", in time of course. Anyway, something like that he was saying. Suddenly I left my seat and ran to the front of the church, where they had an old fashioned mourner's bench. I was weeping and trying to pray. I didn't know what or how, but I was making an effort. How embarrassing it must have been for the congregation to watch an 18 year old loser weeping and sobbing, running to the front of the church. Now, churches often remove the altar or the place of prayer and contrition in the front of the church and they don't have to endure such embarrassing spectacles.

Now my troubles began. Suddenly every time I turned around, I was confronted by myself and what I was. We all know what the favorite phrase of people observing a new Christian say when they catch them in error: "I thought you said that you were a Christian. You are not living up to that statement." I used to think when I heard these words of encouragement, "I never said I was going to be perfect." I was just dumbfounded and tried to get a handle on this new yeast that had thrust itself on my being. It was beyond my understanding and the source of much frustration.

The date of the conversion was July 9, 1950 and by September I was enrolled in college with my brothers. I was accepted on probation in the school only because 2 of my other brothers were going there and Harry was doing well and it was a big hype to have three brothers at the same time. They would give me until December to make good and I had to maintain "C" average. Now, I never had quit reading books. At least one book a week and often more and anything would do. I read cereal boxes, cans, advertisements and etc. The nearest I can explain it to you is the scene from the movie "Short Circuit", where the robot was beating his head on a gas pump and saying, "Input, I need input." When I got to college, they had orientation week and you were given tests to see where you fit. I had failed English in high school and had to take my junior year over as you needed three years of English to graduate. Well, what a shock. The college said I did not need to take English as I had scored so high I would receive credit by examination. Crazy isn't it.

I studied for three years. I spent my time there and graduated. I met a wonderful girl there from a well-to-do home. She was the daughter of an immigrant who had fled religious persecution. I spent many hours talking with him into the wee hours of the night. He spoke several languages, was great with music and well-read and under him, my real education began. His family were jewelers and were moderately wealthy. He came to Wisconsin, to make a living and raise a family on a farm that had its share of swamp land. I once asked him why his family chose such a hard way to make a living. He told me that I did not appreciate my freedoms. To worship as he pleased, to associate as he pleased and to speak his mind as he pleased was all he wanted and the price his family paid for this marvelous freedom was cheap indeed. I loved him as a father.

Some years later they had a family gathering to discuss the inheritance. Gene, my wife's brother-in-law and I were not allowed to attend the meeting. Gene expressed to me his dislike for what was happening and asked how I felt. He said that our families were going to be cut out by greed. I said I don't care, they can have it all. I wanted pops' spiritual inheritance to fall on my children. This has happened. All three of my children are solid in the faith, in spite of me, and even my grandchildren are solid in the faith. For a good man passes his inheritance on to several generations.

I then spent ten years trying to pursue the ministry in small churches until finally I realized I did not fit. I often was asked why I quit the ministry and my standard answer was that my children had picked up a bad habit, they liked to eat. I did everything I could to survive. I worked as a plumber, electrician, hod carrier, brick layer, painter, factory worker, Omar bread salesman, post office worker and anything that would keep a shelter over our heads and place food in the home. I have the tax forms saved yet to show I did all these things.

Finally I was through. Disillusioned, frustrated and full of anger, I left the ministry and Bluffton College took me in. They provided loans, housing and work. The dean looked at my transcripts and said I would receive my Bachelor of Arts degree in liberal arts in one year. I said I was not interested in that stuff anymore, I wanted to pursue science. It was something I could trust. Yeah, I know, text books were still talking about the "ether" as a carrier of radio waves and Mars had canals, as a man's eyeballs staring into the telescope clearly showed. After three years of study in the science realm, I graduated with a science comprehensive major, with emphasis on Chemistry and above all else, Mathematics. I had nearly 100 semester hours in the sciences and still felt ignorant. Before you graduated you took the GREB to enter graduate school. The counselor said I had scored in the ninety-eight percentile in comprehension and ninety-eight percentile on vocabulary. They tried to interest me in going on to graduate school. I thought if I am so smart, why do I still feel so ignorant? I did not believe any of what the test results or the professors were telling me.

I received from the State of Ohio, a teaching permit that said I could teach any math or science curriculum in any high school in Ohio. I was hired to teach Mathematics and I did this for nearly twenty-five years. It was a great experience. There was a problem though. I was frustrated and angry. Migraine headaches would incapacitate me for three days at a time, and I was feeling very violent at times. I went to a doctor I knew and explained to him my problem. I was not going to continue living that way. My children had to put up with me and I found myself working to avoid using violence against anyone. At least this much I was able to achieve the avoidance of violence.

At that time, I did not and still do not believe that paddling achieves a single thing and I still think it is not a way to solve conflicts between parents and children. Later as a superintendant, principal, and Math teacher and in charge of discipline, I refused to paddle. (It seems to me there are two Bible verses that are often taken out of context and everyone seems to know them, even if they attend church casually. The first verse is often quoted as "Spare the rod and spoil the child." The other one concerns women being quiet in church. I sometimes feel like telling them there are better stories you can read in the Good Book).

The doctor set me up with a psychiatrist in a distant city. It would not do to let the school district and parents know I was seeking help of this kind. You could get fired. Still today the public does not like this kind of help. Only my wife and the doctors knew. I went for some time. The doctor made sure there was no medical problem and then he had sessions with me. After some weeks, he said there was no need for me to see him any more as I was a very normal average person. When I asked about the anger he said "that is just a control thing. You need to grow up and discipline yourself." He said that he did not look for any change because I was in a kind of prison, a prison of prisms.

Now, I understand about prisms that refract visible light into its individual colors. This is a well understood phenomenon in science. You have seen the effect when you see a rainbow in the sky. The light passes through raindrops, the water in the raindrops act as one big prism and bends the sunlight into a beautiful rainbow. The point is that the colors are there all the time, but only when the light is acted upon by a prism do you see the spectrum of individual colors.

So, I was a little confused when the doctor was talking about the prisms in my mind. He explained to me that there were mental prisms in the mind which filter my thoughts and help to explain some of my reactions. Real prisms are useful in many ways and are able to show the beauty of a rainbow. But most of the mental prisms in our mind strive against our better self and instead of beauty they show our ugliness. For example, your thoughts bend when they pass through your mental prisms, just as light bends through a prism, so you could envision that instead of the color red, the emotion known as anger shows up, the green component as envy, the yellow as fear or the blue as depression. I know this is a lot of scientific mumbo-jumbo to some, but just think of the mental prisms as devices in our brains that bend and color our perception of reality.

In other words, the use of the concept of mental prisms is just an analogy for how our brain distorts reality and how our emotions, that are always present, are manipulated by our hidden biases. If your bent is towards anger, than every incident, no matter how innocent, can trigger your temper. If you have fear as your filter, it doesn't take much stimulation for you to feel fear in a situation. You allow your prism to tinge and distort your thinking process, and then when you react in a manner that is not consistent with your spiritual desires, you wonder what went wrong.

The doctor explained further that the prisms were tied so closely to my defense mechanisms that it was very unlikely that I would rid myself of them. I had talked in casual conversations with different school counselors about the chances for change in older people and most of them said emphatically that no change was possible after a certain age. Hardening had taken place.

I have enclosed a diagram of what was presented to me. There are different prism bars in each person but some basic ones were in all of us. The diagram represents as closely as possible what was shown to me.

**This shows how the concept
becomes distorted after
passing through the prisms.
(The following page gives
the code for the numbered prisms.)**

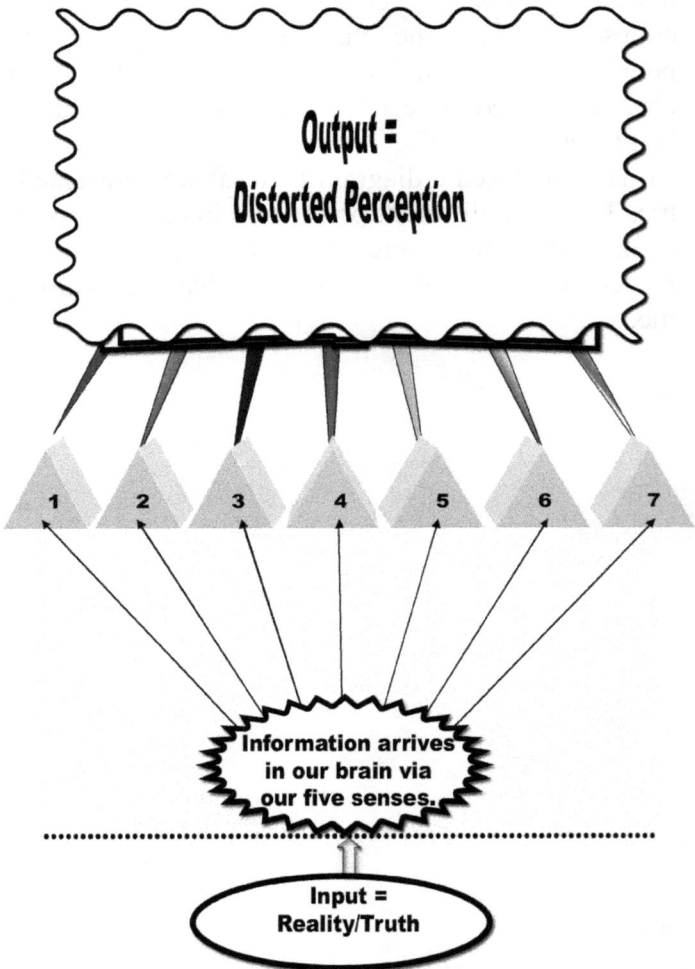

Output =
Distorted Perception

1   2   3   4   5   6   7

**Information arrives
in our brain via
our five senses.**

**Input =
Reality/Truth**

Prism Code

Possible prism contents: Loyalty plays an important part in how intensely you cling to your prisms. Your defense mechanism is tied up in your beliefs, thus affecting your behavior. People have died in defense of these concepts, some of those ideas were based on truth and some were based on lies, at least your understanding of those ideas.

1. Your heritage and what was taught to you about the important things your people believe in. At least your understanding of what they lived and were willing to die for. The parents and the siblings play a major part in this. The lessons of childhood are forever with us and you were of course a child and as such received input of sorts.

2. Your peer group and the culture in the group. What they believe and hold dear.

3. Your religious training or lack of or at least your understanding of religion. Maybe you don't believe anything at all. It all factors in.

4. Your language and how it is used in your culture. No matter what someone is saying, what your understanding of what the word means is the only thing important to you. So we sometimes insult or compliment without meaning to. It's the same with the other person speaking to us.

5. Diet plays a major role. You are what you eat and how you acquire that substance that you intake. When you are desperately hungry, anything may be OK.

6. Education or lack thereof. What you learned will not be violated. Biology, Physics or whatever your money was spent on will not be violated. Anything that challenges your arrival at moment of truth will be distorted or cast aside.

7. Your health at the moment decides the meaning of the concept received.

These are the prisms that I received in 1962 as close as I could remember. I never wrote them down having no intent at the time to write. I was only interested in evolving into a better person. I believe that unless you understand how you think and deal with your personal distortions, there will never be any peace for you in this world.

After much thought, I determined that I could do something about the way I thought. I would find a way to release myself from the prism bars and not hate any part of my heritage. The following diagram represents what measures I took to overcome and release myself from the prison made up of prism bars.

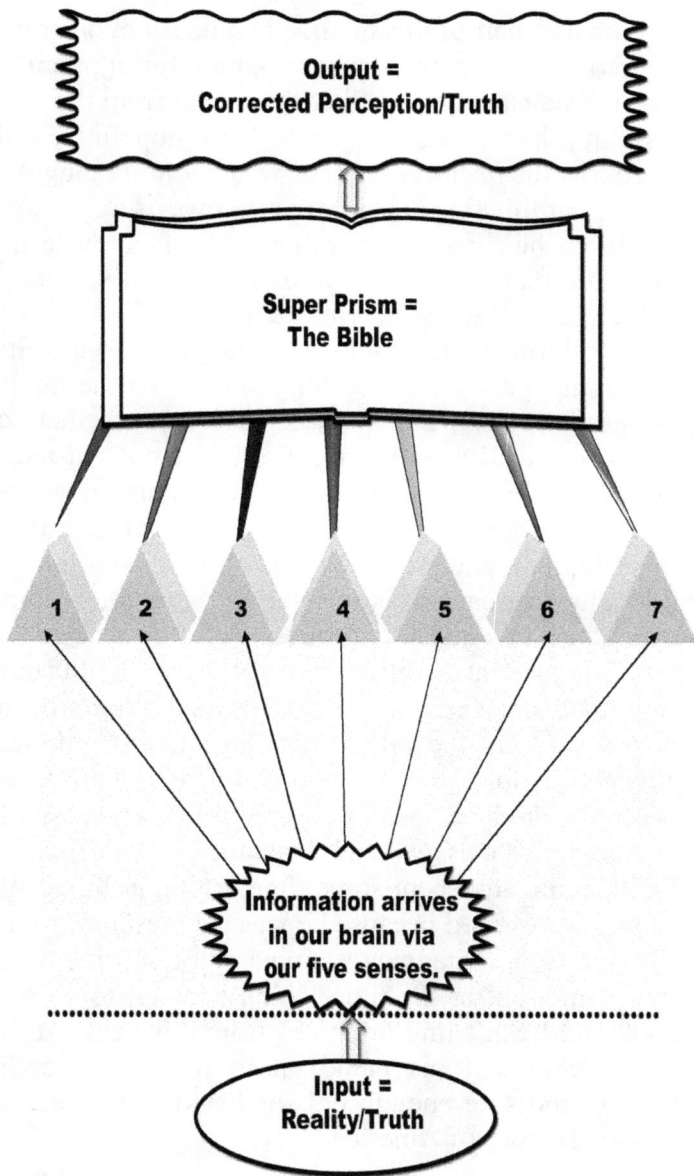

Output =
Corrected Perception/Truth

Super Prism =
The Bible

1 2 3 4 5 6 7

Information arrives
in our brain via
our five senses.

Input =
Reality/Truth

The best part of this method is it does not destroy the proud heritage that makes up our pilgrim prism, but instead causes us to filter the output from the pilgrim prism through the Bible. This, hopefully, will not allow the negative parts of what we were taught to distort our thinking. The process allows us to prioritize the content of our thoughts, so that we can disregard that which is in conflict with God's Word. What is important to us remains important.

The pilgrim prism could be thought of as the first prism, that prism that was formed in us by the family we grew up in, with its entire heritage, whether for good or bad. But with proper priority, we can move ahead without being destructive. If you are alive, you are here because, obviously, many generations preceded you and we owe them some loyalty but not a loyalty that causes us to interpret what we see and experience in a negative fashion.

Let us look at a few ideas that seem to illustrate what damage these strange ingrained programs or prism bars in the mind can do. In 1960 I was attending Bluffton College in Bluffton, Ohio. We were required to take a class in Sociality. While attending this class we had a visiting professor. A Dr. Smith came and spent some time giving lectures. We were quite excited because he was a contributor to the Encyclopedia Britannica. I am sorry I don't know his first name, but at the time I didn't intend to write a book and I can't find my notes from the class. At the time we looked his name up in the encyclopedia records and sure enough he was listed in the section on the "History of America."

Dr Smith said in one of his lectures, that Europe emptied it's streets of the homeless, their thieves and their insane and sent them to our shores. Smith said that the blood line from this menagerie infiltrated our heritage and we are seeing the results. In modern terms, the genetic code in America contains the result of that infiltration. Smith then said, since these were largely oppressed people that were shunted here, they bore in their memory banks a system that could cause us trouble. At the slightest perceived insult Americans want to resort to violence. Smith said therefore whenever our nation will see what they think are oppressed people in some country in the future, we would go shoot the ones we think are the culprits. The persons in America with this genetic code in their blood stream would seek higher office and cause a frenetic action, whenever they perceived what they believe to be injustice anywhere.

Another interesting prism relates to what I read sixty years ago in an anthropology book. I think it was Margaret Mead, although if not, she can't forgive me since she isn't around anymore. She would forgive me if she could. I read the true purpose of war was to weaken, using modern scientific language, the genetic code. We kill off our very best in war. It took the very best to fly a dive bomber or drive tanks, etc. In impoverished and corrupt countries, the persons labeled as criminals, are often heroes. Since they are the ones to stand up to the corrupt government, they could be considered to be the very best their culture could offer. They think and act outside of the box and are systematically imprisoned and are often killed. Therefore, they kill off their very best and brightest.

My own take on this is, if this is so, how we can hope to change other countries that like to kill off their best and thus their genetic code becomes weakened. I read this a long time ago and it makes some sense to me.

Finally, the last prism I will discuss is this one. I have a habit of reading, as I said, everything. In a certain garage where I used to go to have my car repaired, I read many little pamphlets while waiting. I read about flying disks; I read there was no Jewish persecution in World War II, I read the landing on the moon was faked and a lot of other ideas. Hey it's a free press and anything can be written whether it's true or not. At first I was shocked by what was written, but then I thought, no thinking person pays any attention to this nonsense any way. What does that make me?

However one little article intrigued me and I thought I would pass it on. It says that President Eisenhower was wrong when speaking about fearing the military industrial complex. The military industrial complex was a very fine thing, in that it created all kinds of jobs, made a lot of money and helped with the balance of trade. Whenever some nation got to killing one another we could go over, choose a side and help out. When we were done we could use the little war as a marketing tool. When they see how equipment does the job more efficiently then they could buy our equipment and do the job more efficiently. The only problem with this is some other countries are competing with us. They sell their substandard equipment at a cheaper price, this ends up hurting our market.

Well, you should be able to see that there all kinds of prisms in the minds of men and what I suggest is a super prism so we don't get caught up in any of the nonsense. To get a proper perspective of where I am coming from, allow me to say that indeed we are common. We are full of errors and mistakes. We are not the intellectuals, you and I, nor is this intended for those who think that they have arrived. We are the ones that do need help and do seek help.

To better show my approach, I will tell you of an experience I had. When I was about 22, I contracted to lay hardwood floors in new homes. I had contracted to place floors in a large home. A man who had retired and was a master carpenter said he would help as I was on a time frame to get the job done. As we worked, he would work circles around me. An old man, half stove up. I became angry and he caught my anger. He stopped me and said to me that I was a hard head and wouldn't listen to others. He said he was at the top of his craft, but often some ignorant person, who did not know what he knew, would watch him working. They would watch a while and then make some comment as how to do the job better and quicker. He said that he would always stop and listen to the person. He said he had picked up all kinds of short cuts from those that seemed foolish, in other words, those that weren't "experts." He said to me, "When you learn to take good advice without considering the source then there just may be some hope for you."

It took quite a while, but I did profit from what he said. He taught me to look for what seems to be hidden in all those I meet and in what I read. Even though a source might not seem credible to you, you can often pick out a nugget of truth, if you are just willing to listen. Several examples follow of what I have learned from unexpected sources.

*A good example is Ayn Rand. Yes, Ayn Rand, from her writings I have received a better picture of the value of those who create.

*From Lloyd C. Douglass, I learned how to give quietly without anyone knowing. My wife and I are a team, we give and keep quiet.

*From Tielhard, I learned about the environment that I have been placed in and the beauty of what is around me. I learned how important it is to do things correctly; doing as well as one can, with a proper attitude toward work.

*From Gene Stratton Porter, I learned about conservation and how careless we are. We are indeed poor stewards of this marvelous country.

*From Robert Burns, "To a Louse" and "To a Mouse" are my favorite poems and I use them every day of my life to give me proper perspective.

*From Poe and Jack London I learned the value of being a wordsmith. I have tried, but fall so short of their standards. I feel that I am as equivalent to their ability as iron ore is to stainless steel.

I cannot possibly list all the books that have left their mark on me and helped me to assign the proper priorities to my prism bars. I have studied many subjects and I learned enough about these subjects as to know when I should keep my mouth shut. One of these subjects was New Testament Greek, which I studied in college. When interpreting the Bible, I have never said, "The Greek says this or that." There are marvelous students of this subject and the other subjects and I leave it to them. This brings us as to why I use the King James Bible as my master prism. I have a number of translations. I wore out the Weymouth translation. I wore out Phillips' Pauline letters. I was intrigued when he wrote that he felt like he was rewiring an old house and the power was still on. I was brought to feelings of great shame when he wrote that twelve men like the disciples of old, could still change the world, but as he said, there is none of that kind left. I have all most all of the translations. So why do I cherish the King James? The King James Bible, in my opinion and I mean in my opinion, is a book of protest. It is a book of rebellion. The founders of America, Christian or not, used the book to teach themselves and others, the ways to live a better life. It is a book that rebels and protests against tyranny and evil, and when used correctly, insists that you love one another and remove all hate from your life and I like that a lot.

Let's look at merry old England during King James' time. The king, the nobility and the church ruled the land, and death and exile loomed hard in the life of the common man. Come on folks, shake lose of your lethargy and think about it. The king was in a battle with the church at Rome. He had decided that he wanted another wife. He was having an affair with another woman and wanted a divorce. Rome said no, and so the battle was engaged.

The king decided he would place the Bible in the hands of the common man. He would have his own church, the Church of England. So he decreed that the best translators would do the work. Wake up folks.

The translation had to be strictly accurate and had to stand up to the scrutiny of the intellectuals of that time. He was not going to allow a translation that scholars would laugh at. We can imagine the results if the translation were faulty. The authorities of the day, those who had the proper credentials, might decree the book was not accurate. The world would laugh and scoff at the flawed translation. Of course, those doing a shoddy translation would lose their heads. The translation had to be as accurate as possible. It was accurate and met the standards of scholarship. This book has stood the test of time. Christianity, in its heyday, did so much with this translation, and when we decided to use other, more modern translations, little has happened that we could call spiritual. As Phillips said in his translation there are none like the original group left.

Now some modern pastors keep knocking the King James. They don't want a church full of well informed protestors, comparing their sermons to the Book and telling them they are inaccurate. I have even heard preachers say, "Beware of anyone who quotes the King James." I have heard this with my own ears, "The devils", they say, "Know the scripture well, too." Then they complain, "The common man misuses the book and speaks out of context." Bull whackers, they just don't like truth. For my part I am sick of Readers Digest level sermons. The parson says he has spent all week in prayer and study and as a result does not have time to visit with his parishioners. I personally have sat for 45 minutes mentally screaming and saying to myself, "Is this all you got." See, the book does lead to protest.

I need to correct some possible misunderstanding here. I do love Readers' Digest stories. I read their condensed books every time I find one. It takes me about twenty minutes to go through a whole book this way. My mind devours it. I don't mind a Readers Digest level sermon, in fact I love them. I just don't want to hear a sermon at the level of a Readers Digest Condensed Book for more than ten or twelve minutes. To surf on the good will of the audience for forty-five to sixty minutes is a cruelty that is hard to take. This leads me to say that there seems to be a trend toward not practicing the fine craft of composing and delivering a sermon. When I was learning the art of preaching, two of the classes that were important towards that goal were hermeneutics and homiletics. A condensed definition of hermeneutics is the study of interpretations of the Bible. An example of this type of study is examining how Luke's profession as a physician affected his viewpoint as he wrote the Gospel of Luke. The condensed definition of homiletics is the study of rhetoric, or essentially how to construct a sermon. My professor, L. A. Perkins, had a poem that summarized how a well-constructed sermon should flow:

Begin low, speak slow;
Catch fire, rise higher;
When most impressed, be self-possessed;
At the end wax warm, and sit down in a storm.

He had several other pieces of advice; "One climax to a sermon and do not yo-yo your people." The other advice he attributed to Charles Spurgeon, who many agree was one of the best preachers. He would say that 20 minutes was adequate time for a sermon, and more than that was excessive. Additionally, he did not want to hear a sermon unless you had practiced it for at least 10 times. I have since learned that others, who were equally as passionate about instructing the precepts involved with delivering life-impacting sermons, used this poem and gave similar advice.

I have heard many preachers in my long life ranging from those that consistently delivered powerful sermons to those that clearly had no clue about Christianity. I would question those preachers that gave long-winded, wandering sermons about their study of hermeneutics and homiletics. Their replies were all similar: they did not have any use for these subjects and often they took only the bare minimum in these studies just so they could obtain their pastoral degree. They believed that they could be unprepared and still preach a good sermon simply because of their calling to be preachers. Clearly this could be equated to a person who possessed a wonderful talent to play piano, but would eschew any classes or lessons based on the fact that their talent was superior to any they might learn from. The results they would achieve would be limited and probably not worth your time. On the other hand, I have read where great concert pianists practice endlessly and still pursue training in their craft. It is the same with anyone who would strive to be excellent, no matter what talent they are pursuing, and it should be as well with pastors who stand in the pulpit to deliver their message. It is said that one of the great preachers from early in the last century would dress in a tuxedo to preach. He said that he was representing God and wanted to be the best ambassador he could be.

Back in 1957, I was sent to a small church with only 15 regular attendees on Sunday mornings, and that is being generous. I stuck to the schedule of only preaching for 20 minutes. From August of that year to the following March or April, our attendance increased to 150. This was at a time when 150 was an average size church. If I can do this, imagine what someone could do who was loaded with talent. This leads me to say again that I protest. If you have a God-given talent to preach, you need to exercise your talent in order to become proficient at it. Invest some time and effort, practice daily, read as much as you can, and listen to critiques of your sermon even if they seem harsh and irrational. Perhaps you will also be led to a little rebellion; to rebel against that which is tepid and mundane. As Romans 10:14-15 says how beautiful are the feet of them that preach the gospel, so seek to be excellent in how you present the glad tidings of good things. I think that is good advice to all who have been called to follow our Lord and Savior.

Let me give you another prime example of possibly being influenced by rebellion. In merry old England, the common man was taught to read and he lived in his little hovel. He got his hands on the book and he read it with passion. The overseer came by and threatened him. And here is his reply: I have another Lord and you got nothing I want. Throw me out of my house and make me homeless. My Lord will find a pleasant place for me to sleep. In green pastures I will lie down. When I am thirsty, only pure, cool still water will do. You have persecuted me and beaten me down and I have wept in my despair, but every time my LORD has restored my soul. You threaten me with the shadow of death, still I do not fear. My Lord puts on a servant's garments and prepares a table for me. Further when I set down to eat in his presence, he anoints me with oil. He has a manner of discipline that is pleasant to me and I find his rod and staff a comfort. Now you watch me, when I arrive in my own house and look about my community, the people will see only mercy and goodness following wherever my path will lead me. Yes, and then I am going to dwell in His house forever.

When this type of person came to our shores, many of them, but not all, did make sure that their paths contained all the goodness and mercy they were able to muster. Surely you can see that the seeds of freedom planted in the common man by this remarkable book and surely your knowledge of history is good enough to see the truth in what I am saying, and so I will not abandon the Book. Besides dumb as I am, I can understand it, and I have known men who could not read well, yet became skilled at reading with this Book and led fantastic, wonderful, fulfilling lives, because, without realizing it, the Book became an overriding influence in their lives. My father and my mother and several of my siblings after years with the Book, learned how to read well and applying the master prism to their lives, became in time model Christians. The Book is a master prism that does work.

With the previous information given to you, we will look at how free we can be by installing the master prism as our own. I would not dictate that my master prism is yours, I only suggest, as I talk to many successful Christians, they have seemed to, without knowing it, installed the Book as their guide. They have used the King James to override their own ingrained programs and prejudice, programs passed on to them and not of their own making.

A word about plagiarism should be appropriate at this time. When I was in the fifth grade the teacher asked all of the class to each write in their own words a patriotic piece. I did so. Wham, a hand struck me up side of the head and in loud language I was called a cheat. She said no one of my ignorance, could on his own, write those words. She said I was a plagiarist, whatever that meant. She made me place my head on the desk in shame for the balance of the period. I thought to myself, I do not know what this is all about. I asked myself, if I say 2 plus 2 equals 4 does that mean I cheat because someone else said it before me. I resolved never to write anything again. In fact I failed eleventh grade English because I refused to write a piece and read it to the class.

As I approach my eightieth year, I no longer care about the consequences of my actions. I am writing this, so let the critics rave on. Yes, my thoughts are picked up from a myriad number of writers. So what... In my opinion, the original writers are the ones to receive credit and I would freely give it, but having read so much for nearly seventy years, who do I blame for my errant thoughts. What is important is the truth regardless of the source. But as the book of Ecclesiastics tells us so clearly, there is nothing new under the sun.

That being said, I must once again tell you on what basis I come to you. These are the people I have observed and talked to and out of their lives I speak. So I come as a construction worker, a painter, a carpenter, a cement worker, and a host of unnamed men I have worked with who knew Christ and used his Book to clarify their lives and live freely and richly.

What is the manner in which we write? We bring these lessons from these people, who are just like us in so many ways:

*We come to you as Rahab, the harlot, plying her craft, whatever understanding we may have of her. She saved the Israeli spies by hiding them on her rooftop and then helping them escape over the wall of Jericho.

*We come to you as the demonic on the hillside that met the master and had the master excise the evil of lust and greed from his life and let the pigs of the world receive those instruments of destruction, which his own system had once so eagerly embraced. Then these instruments of destruction cause the pigs to drown in their own apathy.

*We come to you as the woman at the well, whose standard of living was to many, appalling, but having met the master she became a missionary for truth and compelled others to come and hear for themselves.

*We come to you as the women caught in adultery and the Master when confronted with the situation simply asked, "Where are your accusers?" And she said, "No one's here." He replied, "I do not condemn you either but change your behavior and take a different path."

*But most of all I come to you as the blind man, who when faced with questions from all of the intelligentsia of the world, said," Well, this one thing I know, I once was blind and now I see."

All of these simple persons have lessons for us that we can use in our daily walk.

The problem with the prisms in our minds is that they are not perfect crystals, but are a collection of half truths, stories and ingrained prejudices, ideas and perceptions with which we have programmed our thought patterns. These defects are the results of many things from our imperfect environment and its interaction with us. They could include our language, inheritance, peer groups and the treatment we receive from others, not the actual treatment, but our perceptions of others' actions towards us. In short our prisms often are made up of a multitude of partial truths. Our prisms are full of distortions; it's like trying to see through a window that is cracked and dirty, you cannot fully see what is on the other side of the glass. All these false impressions tend to bend and warp the truth into something that borders on fantasies, like an actual prism bends and diffracts the light as it passes through it.

So, based on using the King James as my super prism for fifty years, I have been very satisfied by the results. I try to subject every aspect of what I perceive, to be refocused through this Book. I have a more peaceful outlook on life and a better understanding of my fellowman. In fact I have heard so many times people say, Weaver has a scripture verse for everything, and I do, because I have taken the time to study and memorize the King James. It is that important to me. How can you have ill feelings for your fellow men when you understand that they are trying to survive according to the programs or prisms in their mind? Just as I was a victim, so are they. If I can forgive myself for hanging on to false ideas, I can forgive them. Their defense mechanism is tied up in those prisms and they live in fear of new ideas, less some idea leave them vulnerable.

The following lessons are lessons that I use almost every single day, either in part of whole.

Lesson One - Let us begin

Let us begin with Isaiah 1:18: Come now let us reason together says the Lord. Yes, the Lord wants to reason with us. In the process of reasoning with Him, at what must certainly be a very high level, the Lord says we will gain a better appearance. Yes, we will look cleaner, purer and etc. (Of course if we are of the type that does not care how our message of salvation is presented to others, than why worry about our appearance.)

When I first read this passage, as I searched to have a better mind, I was of course shaken and somewhat mystified. A reasoning process with the Lord? That could straighten out a lot of problems and can it even be done? In addition, the Lord indicates that this process of reasoning with Him is a cleansing process. But, how, O Lord, can I reason with you, since the gap between you and me is so immense. I knew that the Lord was not given to raise false hopes in us, so there had to be a way to engage in this process and that is what I began to look for, a way of engaging with my Heavenly Father using my cognitive faculties, a way of interacting with Him that would channel my thoughts into new patterns,

(In an aside, when I got further along in my search for the reasoning process this idea of reasoning together was a fantastic help for me in the class room. It gave me such a fantastic perception of relevance between myself and the student. I reasoned if the Lord could express a desire to reason with me, in spite of the great gap between us, then the gap between me and the so-called least teachable student, in comparison, did not exist. This produced in me, a much better teacher then I would have been without this concept. The behavior of the instructor and attitude of the instructor is more important than that of the student. For the teacher is the yeast, the agent of change in the classroom, for good or for bad.)

I taught Euclidean Geometry for many years and I am not going into the details here of that subject. But one has to use reason, when studying the subject and the first elements one studies are the defined terms, the axioms, and theorems. The axioms are the basic agreements of Euclidean Geometry; they are the building blocks on which the more advanced knowledge of this system rests. In short, in order to communicate your ideas with another person, you both must know the basic agreements. To show you how well reasoning works, mathematicians can spend years studying and arguing amongst themselves about abstract points, lines, planes and dimensions that do not exist, except by agreement. Although we do suspect that such concepts do exist and that three-dimensional space is real. Funny isn't it.

In order for us to reason together, to discuss intelligently and to understand each other, certain agreements have to be made. Just like mathematicians, we have to have a common starting point. There is the rub. I don't think you can find much reasoning in Christianity as practiced today. Perhaps it is my fault, and I am willing to be the blame if that will cure it. But agreement can be had by agreeing on a source that will allow us to converse sensibly. Hint, Hint, how about the Good Book, or is that an unreasonable starting point? As an example of the Bible as the foundation for rational thinking is Proverbs, one of the books in the Bible. Proverbs contains many axioms; it contrasts the difference between wise and foolish behavior. What better place to begin your journey toward truthful thoughts, than learning the wisdom needed to live a godly life? By the way another word for "axiom" is "proverb."

2 Timothy 2:15 is a starting point for reasoning. You must study to show that you are serious about the pursuit of reasoning, study with the purpose of finding the agreements and truths that allow a higher standard of reasoning to prevail. To study is to spend time, examine, explore, investigate, probe, question, research, observe, scrutinize, memorize, jot down notes, read, compare and with careful scrutiny look over your efforts and be sure you do not lose site of the Goal. The goal is to reason in a more effective way.

An old English preacher proposed an equation that fits here in a very effective way. His name was Thomas Bayes. Here is the proposed equation. "INITIAL BELIEFS PLUS NEW OBJECTIVE INFORMATION EQUALS A NEW AND IMPROVED BELIEF." I have read that this equation is really used a lot in working with robots. If you want to read more on this, read a book by Sharon Bertsch McGrayne entitled, "THE THEORY THAT WOULD NOT DIE" Hey! If it works for robots, couldn't it work for us? What a simple equation. Taking where you are mentally, adding new and honest input, results in a better mind. It can be done. Why do we hesitate?

The last thing I would say on the subject of reasoning is the following ideas.

1 Corinthians 2:16 tells us that we have the mind of Christ. This clearly indicates that the mind of Christ is available to us. A few years ago there was a book entitled, "WHAT WOULD JESUS DO." The book was based on the concept that Christ's way of thinking is available to all of us. According to my reading about the book's result, it had a profound effect in the lives of many believers.

Then we have Philippians 2:5 which states, "LET THIS MIND BE IN YOU, WHICH WAS ALSO IN CHRIST JESUS." Wow, and wow again. There are three things, at least, explicit in these verses:

One-The mind of Christ is readily available.

Two-The verses certify that the action of letting the mind of Christ dwell in us, can be done.

Three-There is something in us that is impeding the action from taking place.

Now to let something happen is to not only give permission for this to happen, but we have to take action and unlock the vault of the heart and mind, so the change can take place. It means we have to abandon any thinking that causes unwarranted anger, mistrust, and suspicion of others and we do that by letting the mind of Christ penetrate into the depths of our being. The choice, of course, is always ours, but clearly we can see the responsibility is ours and the results one way or another is our just reward. It will happen to us as we choose and we deserve what we get.

Lesson Two - We now take up the subject of God

We now take up the subject of God, and we do so with great anxiety and care. This is one place I do not want any distortions because of my own limited ability. The ancient Hebrew, I am told, would not use the name of God in casual conversations, but substituted other references generally understood by their peers. In the same way, I do not use His name if I can help it, because it is too easy to take His name in vain. I hope you understand what I am referring to. Persons will say, "God told me to do this," or "God told me to do that." Whenever I hear these words, I shudder a little. The area where the name of God is often used in vain, it seems to me, is in the arena of prayer. In a group of persons, I once remarked, "People seem to think that The Almighty is the great udder in the sky, and with proper massaging by tears, groans and acts of charity, the heavens will open and good things will come rushing down." This was not well received.

Emily Dickinson said it so well in a little poem she wrote about prayer:

> Of Course I prayed
> And did God Care?
> He cared as much as on the Air
> A Bird had stamped her foot
> And cried "Give Me"

She seems to infer that there is more to prayer than a simple "give me."

There is a certain terror in me about using God's name in vain. Though it may happen, my intent is not to do so. In my zeal towards my Lord, I have uttered prayers every day at some time or other for nearly thirty years. During these prayers, I made sure, if I could, to not use His name in a vain manner. Many times during the day, but most often in the morning when the day begins, I breathe this type of prayer. I rarely ask for anything specific. I don't need to be specific. This is because of the promise found in Luke, the twelfth chapter. In this passage, Jesus is talking about God's provisions for the birds of the air and ends with the promise that God will take care of our needs as well.

Please forgive me if I seem to be critical of anyone's prayer life. This is not my intention. I am merely stating that care must be made to not offend the one to whom we address our prayers.

My prayers conform to the following pattern: "Help!" After this, I am reasonably sure that the person seated on the throne and surrounded by the ten thousand times ten thousand says, "Somebody help the boy." Then, I follow up with the following (these words fit my view and may not fit yours): "Help me, oh God! Visit me not in your hot displeasure, but rather have mercy on me. I am truly sorry for the ways I have offended Thee, and please, My Father, have mercy on me. I detest all my sins, because I dread the loss of heaven and eternal separation from thee. I fear the fires of hell, because of the company that I must keep and the ensuing pain. More than anything else I am sorry for offending Thee, Who art all Good and deserving of all my love and gratitude."

This prayer, of course, is based on a prayer of contrition that the Catholic Church offers, if I am correct. You see, whether good or bad, source means nothing. Truth means everything.

Based on these thoughts, I have therefore coined or use other names when I speak of the Almighty, and I will use them sometimes in this book as I do in life. Naturally, there is the name Almighty. The other names I use are: the Creator, Love, or the most frequent name I use in my personal life, but may not appear very often in other places, is "The Personal Energy Force of All the Dimensions Known or unknown to humans." I supposed the name most often used is MY Lord. I cannot define God. Neither can I humanly have any concrete perceptions of the personal Energy force. Doing so would mean that humans are able to define parameters for the Almighty. I know He is love, He creates, He has a personality, and He has emotions. Also, I believe that He is personally interested in each individual soul, along with that soul's progress toward His being.

The reason I like these new names, is that it is virtually impossible, unless you really work at it, to blaspheme or take the names of the Creator in vain. Go ahead, and you will see that you cannot curse very well using the name of Love. As we know the basic concept of mathematics that $1 = 1$, so we should know that God equals love. We are told this in the Book. God is love is the original axiom. This is the first concept that we have to agree with, for it is the basic building block for all of life. If we do not agree with this axiom, then we will have not gained a foundation for rational thinking and our ability to reason will be impaired.

So lesson two, out of necessity, is short. You can do your own search for Him, and apparently He is not all that difficult to find. Romans 10:20 states that God was even found by those who were not even seeking Him. If the finding of God can be accidental in some cases, what happens if we seek "The Personal Energy Force of All the Dimensions Known or unknown to humans" and seek Him with a purpose?

Hebrews 11:6 gives us the clue to the search and why many persons have not found God. It says that he that comes to God must believe that He is, and that there is a reward for them that DILIGENTLY seek Him. Who are you kidding when you say you can't find Him? You wouldn't cross the United States as a forty-niner looking for gold if you did not think it existed, but all of the gold in the world does not even compare to the value of your soul. So, since you possess something far greater than all the treasures on the earth, why not spend the effort to get to know the Creator of your soul?

Enough said.

Lesson Three - A brief interlude into speculations

Before we go on, I must deviate a bit. Sometimes a little levity in a kind way may do us good; a brief interlude into speculations. It would be easy for me to believe in a godless evolution based on the evidence at hand. First, there is the matter of language. Now, for this purpose, I am role-playing as one that believes in evolutionism. In my mind, the ancient Greeks were at the apex of human evolution. They had different words that meant love, and there was no mistaking which type of love they had in mind when they were communicating with each other. They had a word for a father's love, a mother's love, and so on. Now over time, our language has certainly deteriorated, and our ability to express ourselves to one another has gone downhill. Look at the letters ordinary Civil War men wrote home; how eloquent they were.

Not only language, but when a bunch of men molest an eleven year old girl and say it was her fault, it gives undisputed evidence of humans going downhill. An atheist would say there is no god and those humans were therefore exercising their right to live well.

So let us agree on the following assumptions, still role-playing as one who is an evolutionist:

*The concept of entropy, whereby nature tends to move from an ordered system to an unordered system.

*The current degenerate state of our world

*There is no higher power

From these observations, we can see that apparently the evolutionary pendulum has swung back in the negative direction, and very rapidly during my life time. Soon, if time continues on, three or four thousand years from now the pendulum of evolution will swing so far back our descendants will be scratching each other looking for protein in the form of fleas.

Since I am not an atheist, I had better get on with what I need to do. I will now use new words for love to distinguish the difference. For love of the Personal Energy Force, I use "PEFLOVE." For the false love that some humans consider as love, I use "clove", or control love. Let me give you an example of "clove": if you are born in a family that is moderately civil, they will say we love you. This, they think, is their ticket into your life. They feel that by virtue of their statements, they are now entitled to control you. This is their idea of love. They say, "You are in my environment and I have said I love you." You are now expected to respond to this great love and sacrifice by conducting yourself in a manner that pleases them. Should your actions be such that are not to the lovers' liking, much guttural noise may be made that may correctly be interpreted as meaning for you to lay down in abject fear and apologize to them. In other words, they place limits or constraints on their love. But true love, according to I Corinthians 13, has no bounds.

When "Peflove" makes the statement, "Love not the world", He is saying do not try to "clove," or control, the world. There is of course "dlove" for father, "mlove" for mother, "blove" for brother, "slove" for sister, "flove" for fraternal love, etc... Now, I may not be more civilized, but I feel as if I am. I actually will not use these substitutes, but this will give you a better idea of how hard it is to take an idea and recreate it in another human's mind. Our abstract ideas of love are difficult to communicate to others, and just as hard to understand from them as well. We have destroyed our language, and with it has gone a lot of our ability to be reasonable with each other.

Humans like to "clove" the world. They destroy the forests, the animals, the lakes and rivers, and drain the oceans of their vitality. This is what I believe "The Person Energy Force of the Universe" is saying when we are instructed to not love the world. Personal Energy Force, God, says in John 3:16 that He so loved the world that He was willing to pay a personal price for it. Clearly, clearly, we need to have fine reasoning powers to reason as He reasons. This may be our working out of our salvation with fear and a kind of terror. The love that He is presenting is the unidentified, much sought for energy force of the universe. The "string" in the string theory, the "unifier" in the unified field theory, the "everything" in the theory of everything... you get the picture.

Lesson Four - The idea of "not God"

When we speak of God, we also need to consider another aspect of the matter: the idea of "not God" or that God does not exist. We have to admit that there are those persons that say there is no God, they call themselves atheists. I can't say they have a legitimate argument for their statement that there is no God. They just say so, but saying so doesn't make it true. You get nowhere arguing with this type of person for there is no basis, as we have stated earlier, for us to reason together. There has to be some agreements, but rather I have found them to be all too disagreeable. Now, I have had some fun with them on occasion, but I no longer take the time to bandy with them. Their arguments remind me of the old medieval contention that had intellectuals debating how many angels could dance on the point of a needle, which is pretty pointless. Nevertheless, they are alive, and my belief tells me there is only one thing necessary for me to acknowledge them: that they are alive and God has made the decision that I must care for them. I will show you a couple ideas from my view point.

Once, a long time ago, when I was having too much fun intellectually, I used to bandy with an atheist whenever I found one. In this one instance, a person working with genetics said to me, "Weaver, what are you going to think when we, using our scientific knowledge, create life and then human beings?" I said, "I will be surprised if you do not do just that thing you are talking about. In doing so, you will have confirmed what the Book says essentially: an intelligent mind, with full scientific ability, originally created life and then man. So hurry up with the confirmation process." He walked away muttering something about idiots. Well, I confess.

In another instance, a biologist who deemed himself to be an atheist said, "Weaver, you are ignorant for believing that tripe." I rose to the occasion and said, "If you don't believe there is a God, why are you going to great lengths to do what He told you do to? The original orders to Adam were to name all of the animals. You are going to places of great danger, exposing yourself to all kinds of rigor, mosquitoes, swamps and what not, doing what God said you have to do. You can't help yourself; you are obeying the orders of a God you say does not exist." Once again, I heard disgusting words about such nonsense that ended with him saying, "You can't make sense with an idiot." Again, I confess, and, maybe so.

To be honest, it is easy for me to believe there is a God. What is difficult for me is to believe that man exists. However, I am faced with a modicum of evidence. Allow me to tell a little story to illustrate this. In another dimension, perhaps the tenth or eleventh, two individuals who had not seen each other for some time met in an outdoor café for a cup of coffee. (I believe in all of the dimensions there are outdoor coffee cafés). Their names were Hart and Tac. After the appropriate round of handshakes and I'm okay and you're okay, they sat down to talk. Hart begins by saying, "Where have you been Tac? I haven't seen you for a few ages." (There is no time in their dimension, but we have to make do the best we can). "Well, Hart, I found a wormhole, and through it

I traveled to a third dimension." "Tac, you have spent too much time in Professor Idits class. If you remember, I went to that class with you. You know Tac, they carted him away because he said there was a dimension where strange things happened." "Well Hart, he was right, all the way down to the chart he had on the wall. I saw inanimate materials like iron and sulfur, and a whole lot of other elements. Then Hart, these materials joined together and became moving, creating, destroying, and sensing beings. These beings were doing all kinds of things: they would get together, talk together, make a decision, and then with their word as a blueprint, they would do whatever they set out to do." "Now Tac, you have carried this much too far. If the ones in charge found out what you are saying, they would cart you away too. You are describing a dimension full of gods." "Hart, I am not surprised that you don't believe these gods exist. Why, they themselves have a group of people who don't believe they exist either. Their own writings say there is no god."

One final little story to illustrate the hopelessness of no God. This is a takeoff of a story I read in the distant past, but I can't find it and I would like to give credit. Once upon a time there was no dimension at all, and no point. Space could not be conceived by anything, since there was nothing around to conceive it. The powers that be chose to insert a point into space. In this way, conception began, sort of.

Well, the powers that be seeing the poor little point was so alone, created another point to share space with it. Now, real conception began with a crescendo. Points between the points instantly appeared so fast that rabbits would have held their heads in shame had they been aware of what was happening. Now churches sprang up: there was the church of the straight line, the church of the curved line, and there were points with no beliefs at all. They all were busily creating an instantly, infinite number of points between any two points that could be found. One little point, tired of all the fuss and arguments, managed to leave the one dimension and wandered away in space. Instantly, two dimensions came into being and flat land appeared.

Now, the churches began to fold up since there was no sense in arguing. Besides, there was the matter of important stuff like filling flatland with a lot of other points. After a while, one little point was bored with all of it and left flatland. Suddenly, the third dimension came into being. Now, old manuscripts and artifacts were dug up. The churches were revived, along with the old arguments from before.

Stop! Stop!!! This story is really pointless. What's the point? The story is as pointless as the future world of the unbeliever. A world where entropy wins, and the pointlessness of all they believe in comes to full fruition with the morbid realization of their meaningless life. I don't adhere to that world. I believe, and I hope. Even though I have no scientific proof to satisfy persons that have those demands, my world is full of joy and the records of love, charity, and heroism will go on. I confess that this hope of mine, a very thin margin of hope, is that this book will help someone. I would not have ventured into this effort at all except for my desire to be of help.

Lesson Five - We now consider the Virgin Birth

We will now consider the Virgin Birth. What a remarkable story it is, and the lessons the story teaches are the profoundest of the profound. The story is one full of mystery, doubt, faith, the supernatural, correction, and healing. The Lord, of whom I consider to be the greatest deviser of mysteries and enigmas, has provided hidden clues to the mystery, so that you really have to be at the top of your game to find the kernels of truth hidden within it. You cannot even get to the full story, without going back to the story of Garden of Eden. To help us, I will use a family setting. The persons of this family are named Willie, Elvira, and little Sammy. I use this family because in my 60+ years of search for God, I have met individuals like these who have been of the utmost help to me. I have found that persons who have been treated in the most horrible ways and are still able to have joy, a smile, and laughter, are people with outstanding reasoning ability. Only an outstanding mind could put up with the idiocy that has been heaped upon their heads and still survive happy. As a matter of fact, I have known people just like those in this family, though I will not tell you who they are and where they live. If you have the brains God gave a duck, you can find them yourself.

Our story begins with Sammy coming home from Sunday school. He is regaling his father and mother with what he has learned about the story that takes place in the Garden of Eden. Although the teacher is of the highest order, Elvira feels that there are some things that will help Sammy better understand the story. Elvira has asked Willie to take Sammy aside and tell the story as she and Willie have often discussed it, and Willie has agreed to do so.

Willie says, "Sammy, lets you and I go over the story. We can add a few points, and sort of fill in some gaps in our understanding. There seems to be some confusion, Sammy. The garden was nice and fine, and maybe the living was easy, but it was not perfect. Sammy, there was evil in the garden, or else old man Satan was a nice guy. You see, he was there wandering around and being deceptive. When you have deceit present in an environment, one could say that evil is there as well. Adam and Eve were not bothered about the imperfections, for they did not know the difference between good and evil yet."

"Now, there was death in the garden too. If it was not so, then Adam would not have known what the Lord was talking about when He said, 'When you eat of that tree, you will die.' Sammy, there was a lot of gaps in Adams knowledge, but Adam knew more than enough to get by and do well. And the Lord enjoyed talking to Adam and visiting with him. What a wonderful thing to have happened to a person to have the Lord himself walking and talking and being the guide in the garden by pointing this and that out. Just like you, Sammy, Adam was going to Sunday school, and the Lord Himself was the teacher. So, we know that when Adam sinned, he surely knew enough to understand that the Lord was right in telling him what he should and shouldn't do. You see, Sammy, the first lesson in doing what is right is to be obedient. The Lord liked Adam to be busy, so he gave him a job to do. Adam was supposed to be a steward in the Garden and name all the animals and look after them. If we read carefully, Sammy, we see that The Lord liked what he had made, and man was given the responsibility to take care of his environment."

"Now, man is very thoughtless and careless, Sammy, for all through the Good Book the Lord keeps talking about responsibility. You remember when your friends laughed at the story of Noah and said, 'How can they get all those animals get into the ark?', and how your mother explained that the story was kind of a prophecy. She said that the ark was the earth, and once again the Lord is teaching us responsibility. We have people today that can't understand how all these things get stuffed into this little ark called earth. Sammy, in Psalm 8, the Lord is telling man, once again, that he is in charge and what animals man decides to keep around, by being careful, will be here. What man is careless with, will not be here. The Lord was a great environmentalist, and His people ought to be in the front taking care of the environment."

Elvira steps in and says, "Willie, you are spending too much time and not telling the story. Quit drifting around and get to the story. The poor boy has to go to sleep soon."

"Anyways, Sammy, the Lord says in the Book that there are ten thousand times ten thousand surrounding the throne, and that these beings just might be a lot smarter than we are and they might be a whole lot more powerful then we are. So when the Lord gives His word and says something, we can imagine a whole lot of action taking place. The Lord said,

'Adam is working very hard doing what I told him, so let's get him some help.' Now, the Lord took part of Adam and made a helper. Sammy, when the Lord sends help, He always sends the very best. There is a reason the Lord used Adam to make this new creature in his environment, Sammy. When the mother sheep has had a little one, we see how they sniff each other and get to know each other. They both know they belong to each other, because they know that they are both part of each other. So, when this new creature called Eve appeared on the scene, Adam was quite comfortable about the addition. He didn't shun her for they both knew they were part of each other."

"So Adam and Eve were walking and living in the garden, and they were flesh but no sin was there, so the Lord was pleased to walk and talk with these beings in the flesh. Sammy, this should put to rest the idea that the flesh is sin, and is the cause of sin. The Lord says that the flesh is weak, but he is not saying the flesh is not strong by itself. Although, when the flesh comes up against the spirit and the mind, why the flesh doesn't stand a chance. Men are always saying that the flesh of the woman is the cause of their misbehavior, but like Adam before, they persist in a lie. Sammy, Ephesians 6:12 tells us very clearly that the struggle is not with the flesh. Our struggle is always in the mind and with the spirits that reside in the world."

"Now, Satan was in the garden and he decides to use the worst of all sins, deceit. He does this to deprive the persons in the garden of their rightful position. He wants to rob them of something very valuable, their inheritance through the Son. We know that even today there are groups of persons in certain businesses that, through deceit, want to throw people out of their homes and acquire for themselves the rightful property of others."

"So Satan sees Eve, and using guile and much talk he says, 'I have been watching you, and you haven't eaten of that one tree. In fact, you have been avoiding it.' Eve says, 'I have been told not to, because at the time I eat of that tree I am going to die.' Satan replies, 'You are not going to die, but you will know the difference between good and evil.' So, Eve takes council from an ungodly source, just like the Psalm 1:1 says not to, and she eats of the tree."

"We know what happens next, Sammy. Eve is going around, maybe singing 'I ate of the tree and I didn't die. I ate of the tree and I didn't die.' Now, all of a sudden she is a lot smarter than Adam, for she now knows about good and evil and Adam doesn't. The Lord did not come down and judge her right away. She is still in the garden and she has not been kicked out yet. Sammy, the Lord is a reasonable friend and does not act rashly but will give us time to repent."

"Now, Adam comes on the scene, and they have a little conversation. When Adam saw, and understood, what went on, he, with full knowledge of what he was doing, willfully disobeyed and ate of the tree. All of a sudden, things begin to look different and he looks at Eve with his new mind (he sees Eve and he says and thinks some things differently). Right away they become ashamed and make clothing for themselves, maybe because of the new thought life now that they knew about good and evil. And then they hide themselves, which always takes place naturally when we have done something we shouldn't have."

"Sammy, things get a little hot now, and maybe they start to sweat a little. They hide out in their foolishness, thinking that the Lord, who sees and knows everything, doesn't know what's going on. Now, the Lord, being very wise and not wanting to make matters worse, waits until things cool down a little, which is always the wise thing to do. He comes down and asks a few questions like 'Why are you hiding?' Adam makes a statement about being naked and ashamed. The truth came out, as it often does, that he had partaken of the fruit of the tree of knowledge of good and evil. Still, they are not kicked out of the garden, and judgment is still being withheld. It is important to listen to explanations of reasons why, even though we know that the reasoning will be faulty."

"Now Sammy, opportunity presented itself and Adam instead makes a huge mistake. He does not confess his sins, but blames his sin on someone else. The person he blames it on is the great gift the Lord had given to him. Sammy, you know how Miss Smith next door planned all year to buy a gift for her husband's birthday. She saved her few dollars that she could for one full year. You know how she would come over and she and your mother would sit in the kitchen and plan and giggle and laugh about what Miss Smith was going to do. Well, the day came and the gift was given. Old man Smith looked at the present, slammed it on the floor, and stomped out of the house. Your mother saw Miss Smith on her back porch weeping with great shudders of her little frame, and your mother went over and tried to comfort her weeping together. Now, you know the anger that came out of that, and we can imagine what happened when Adam refused to confess his sin and blamed the Lord for giving the great gift. Well, the Lord said 'That's it, you are out of here and that sweat you learned about when you did wrong, why you are going to see a lot more of it."

Sammy says to his father, "Daddy I think I know what you are talking about. When I make a mistake and do wrong, I will try not to blame someone else. I will try to confess my wrong doing and ask you to help." Willie says, "If you have a willing mind to do that, why you are acceptable to me as you are and not as you are not. Good night Sammy." "Good night mommy and daddy."

What you may ask does all this have to do with the virgin birth? The virgin birth has to do with the true source of sin, as well as what is sin and what is not. The virgin birth is about stewardship, faith, the supernatural, and valuing the things that the magnificent Father has placed in our environment; the things of value He has given us. I have no intention of beating this to pieces, and it would take several books to slam dunk the concept. After all that, we still would not acknowledge and believe. I have not the time in this book to tell you about Deborah, Ruth, Naomi, Lydia, and a host of persons whose lessons of their lives enriches our Knowledge of the dimension where God the Father resides.

Though, we must talk about little Esther. The great minds of Israel had taken the ship of Israel and had run the ship on the rocks through their foolishness.

Israel was about to be vanished from the good Earth, and this little slip of a girl subjected her will for the common good. Through her enterprise, sacrifice, and wisdom, she entered the place that was forbidden in the law, touched the unclean things, and single handily salvaged the ship of Israel from the rocks through a great act.

The next person we consider is Sarah. What a magnificent person. She was the wife of Abraham, and while Abraham was busy fraternizing with the help, she remained faithful. After waiting a long time, she became pregnant with a son. She taught me that dreams become goals, and goals can be realized when we put whatever assets we have to our dreams. All she had was herself, and she gave what she had to pay the price and fulfill the dream.

I have told her story many times to whoever would listen. I have never been able to tell the story without weeping, and even now, I am offering up tears to pay homage to this great lady. She was old, lived in a desert community, and made her bed on a mat. I picture Sarah's body swelling and weak with age, struggling to get up from the mat in the morning, while a maid and her son made fun of Sarah. Her husband apparently did nothing to stop the treatment, for it continued on when the son was born. It finally came to full fruition when Sarah, right or wrong, had had enough and said you're out of here to the maid and her son. I can picture Sarah in the final trimester of birthing, heavy with child, working to stand erect from the mat. She was walking with a stick of some sort, groaning with pain, and calling on her God for strength to bear the child. Yes, she gets mentioned in the faith chapter of Hebrews where it says, through faith, Sarah received the strength to bear the child of her dreams. She brought whatever assets she had to the task and transformed the dream into reality. Because of her, the lineage continued on and Christ was born of Mary.

Sarah taught me my favorite prayer which I pray every day, many times each day. Help!!! I believe that the Divine, sitting on His throne, hears and says to ten thousand times ten thousand beings surrounding the throne, "Somebody help them." There, I have said it again.

We have one more lady to consider before the grand finish featuring the birth of the Christ Child. For nearly fifty years, I would read one chapter in the Old Testament, one chapter in the New, one Psalm, and one chapter in Proverbs. This I would do every single day. On the thirty first day, I would read the thirty-first chapter of Proverbs. I once told a preacher about my efforts, and he said, "If you have done this for so long, how come you are so far behind spiritually?" I replied, "Some persons, like myself, are special cases and need more help." I admit, I had to chuckle when I once read in a modern translation of Proverbs 31, give beer to the people. (I still think they should buy beer themselves) I am filled with remorse, maybe so or maybe not, for injecting a little pun in this place of seriousness.

The story of the lady described in Proverbs 31 tells of a woman that cannot be bought. You would never have enough wealth. Yes, you may be able to buy the body, but the essence of her being is not for sale. She is a person of high integrity. She gets up a great while before day, and her candle stays bright after dark. Her children and her servants are well fed, and wear fine garments. These things are the products of her mind and efforts, but it is not just her hard work that sets her apart and brings out her worth, she is an entrepreneur. With her mind, she sees a field and buys it with her savings. No one is giving this fine lady anything. She saves more money and plants the field, and then she is in business. Out of seemingly nothing she produces wealth, security, and happiness in her environment.

Let's look at her husband; what a busy fellow he is. He sleeps snoring on his bed. In the morning, a gentle hand touches his shoulder and a soft melodic voice causes him to rouse from his slumber. Perhaps a cup of tea is placed in his hand and he sets up and sips from it. He hears the voice telling him that breakfast is ready, dear. He arises, performs his toiletry, and strides to the table which is set with the bounty of her hands. He arises from the repast and dons the fine clothing she has made him. He places his cap on his head and strides from the home. With his staff, he strides down the street, and since he is a pleasant chap, he nods to all he sees. He hears the whispers that ask, "Who is that?", and he hears those who reply saying, "Why that is Ms. Smith's husband. What a lucky person he is." Perhaps he grins a little and strides on. Where is he going to work? Why, he is going to sit on his backside all day in the city judgment seat handing out advice, as well he should. Any son of Adam that has the good sense to marry such a woman should be handing out advice. What does this have to do with the virgin birth? Everything.

We are talking about value, about integrity, and about righteousness.

We, of course, have arrived at the crescendo of the message from God to man. This is the apex, the highest mountain peak, the overture. Let us imagine back to that night, in the dark black thickness of man's night. It is a quiet, still night, a night like those that preceded it: mundane, tiresome, and hopeless. Suddenly, there are an untold number of spurts of light flashing from the mouth of a number of untold cannons. The dark night is shocked by the thunderous roar. The reverberations echo back and forth through the hills, the light illuminates even the elements of the atmosphere. Then, the sound of wondrous music fills your ears accompanied by the glaring flashes from the arrival of an immeasurable number of angels. The night is suddenly aglow, brighter than the hottest star and whiter than the most blistering blast furnace as the voice of God thunders across the ages His favorite message, To you, sons of Adam, comes this blessed gift. The gift of the woman that I gave to you, O Man, whom you have blamed for your original, willful transgression, she has brought forth from her flesh, and her immaculately pure mind, the person that will rescue you and your race.

She has produced the Savior, your way of escape.

I am trying to move very carefully as I proceed with this story, though there are a few things to add. To complete the analogy of the story, I would like to look at what took place with as honest an eye as this heart of mine can produce. Mary and Joseph were required to return to his home town and he took with him his espoused wife. They were not married. When they returned to the home town, we would not be surprised at what may have taken place.

The young girl was large. I well remember what happened to young ladies sixty or seventy years ago who were caught in an awkward situation. I lived with my grandmother for a number of years. We sometimes talked about the terrible ways people acted. In the 1890's, she was a midwife in her community, and she was not happy with the way people treated each other in times of stress. I think of the situation of this young lady about to give birth: no room in the inn, no relative to take her in, no stranger who would take care of her in her moment of extreme pain and discomfort, no midwife to help. Instead, she went to a place were animals were housed. This is in olden times, not in modern barns of wealth. The odors of the place... She brought forth the child, and without the benefit of perfectly disinfected clothing, she wrapped the child with what she had, and laid him to rest where the animals had their feed.

There are so many lessons in this story.

One: The flesh, in and of itself, is not sin, but rather coupled with a pure mind, is capable of producing sinless perfection.

Two: Women, children of Adam, are not inferior to men.

Three: Man is responsible for his own actions and not the actions of others, no matter the gender, age, race, etc...

Four: Sin comes through an inherit tendency from the sons of Adam.

Five: If you want something of pure integrity, no man is allowed.

In chapter seven of Romans, Paul explains that in the flesh, there is a mind in man that is somehow coupled with the weakness of the flesh, and is stronger than the will of man. We are just naturally disposed to sin. The sin nature (so called) is an inherited tendency, and likes to be disobedient to the law of God.

There are, of course, many other lessons for us. We could not exhaust them all. We can consider a situation where a person is in a coma. They might be a one-year-old or someone in their 90's. As long as they lay in the coma, they are not committing acts of sin. Activate the mind, and perhaps as the mind begins to want something, then you could see acts that could be considered sin. So, we can see it is the mind coupled with "I want" that begins the act of sin. Even if you are of the persuasion that divinity was not involved, at least you should have the grace to remove the negative judgments of people caught in their hour of distress. Just the humanity of man alone calls for compassion.

I CANNOT TELL YOU HOW THIS YOUNG GIRL'S SITUATION BROKE MY HEART. I believe that divinity was uniquely involved in Mary's story. Joy overcomes the sad pathos that could fill my heart without God.

I do not watch much television. I do admit to watching the weather forecast and nature shows. The one program that my wife and I enjoy is a morning news show with an informal format. When the co-hosts and their regular guests are all together in person, the set hums with reasoning. You have persons with widely different viewpoints; with fine intellects sitting around exchanging ideas without any bitterness, allowing each to state their view points. This cannot be happening. Why, they appear to respect each other in our America of the brave and the true.

I did sit up from my chair and was in a state of wonderment when they had an individual talking about his views on the virgin birth. I found it hard to keep from laughing at the individual. His argument was the ancient Hebrew text says "maiden" and not "virgin." I said to my wife, 'What is he saying?" Is he saying because the word is 'maiden' and not 'virgin', divinity was not involved in the birth of Our Lord? Is he suggesting that the maidens of Israel, who were in an unmarried state and in a home that is highly sheltered by a set of parents that have a great zeal for their God, were not virgins? Is he saying that the maidens of Israel would slip out behind the shed and indulge in misbehavior? This person is fortunate to be living in modern America and not in ancient Israel. Just imagine the situation: an Israelite father has said his unmarried daughter, raised in a secure, sheltered environment, was a maiden, but another person replied that his daughter wasn't necessarily a virgin just because she was a maiden. That ossified wag would find himself looking out through a pile of stones.

Besides, the point is, a girl child in a state of innocence, with an immaculately pure mind, could have brought forth perfection, if she did not have the benefit of one of the sons of Adam. God didn't need a son of Adam to birth perfection. Even though the sons of Adam tend to think the world revolves around them. In the Hebrew tradition, if your mother was a Jew, than you were a Jew and thus a rightful heir. This is my understanding of the matter, therefore the possibility exists that I am an adopted son of God because my Savior's mother was a Jew.

On one final note in this lesson, I believe in the virgin birth. I believe that when this young lady became of a certain age, the first egg she produced, through the intervention of the divine, began to grow and went through haploid and diploid cell division and growth. I believe that the modern scientist, while doubting the virgin birth, is trying to duplicate it. Examine attempts at cloning and other experiments. I believe that they may succeed. I believe if they do, they will create their dream, the monster of Frankenstein. Just as God, through Mary, caused Jesus to be born in His remarkable image, so man will create a being in his own image with all of the hate and malice that he is capable of producing, if he is successful. Now, the person who says there is no God, will then become what he insists does not exist, a god. He will thus prove the lie to those who say there are no gods.

Lesson Six - Communication through Civil Reasoning

I have chosen to call this section "Communication through Civil Reasoning", though I have failed at this on occasion. I have heard persons of my persuasion on occasion state, "We need to return to our early Christian roots." To do this, I sometimes feel we really don't have to go too far. Paul, in 1 Corinthians 1:10-18, is concerned about contentious behavior, and, to be honest, we seem to like contention more than we like unity.

To be civil is to fundamentally be concerned with the rights of others. To present ourselves in rude behavior obscures the truth of anything we wish to present. Colossians 4:6 states: Let your speech be always with grace, seasoned with salt, that you may know how you ought to answer. In I Peter 3:15-16: But sanctify the Lord God in your hearts: and be ready always to give an answer to every man that asks you about your reason of hope. And we should answer with meekness and fear. He further says that our conversation should be good.

Civics has its roots in the word civil, and you can't have civilization with a lack of civil behavior. This is what the study of civics is all about. I don't mean to pick on teachers, but it does show when teachers want to impart a message, they are excellent. What concerns me is that in the realm of faith, we seem to take the same approach and wonder about our results. The danger in using examples is they are not completely accurate, but sometimes they are close enough. The reason for this section is simple: Philips says in his translation that 11 men changed a world worse than ours. He also suggests that this type of person is no longer around. I want to examine the plausible reasons, and I think that the root of the problem just may be unreasoning attitudes. This results in a lack of civility, and is accompanied by an overabundance of rudeness.

I am not surprised when the results of the lack of civility in the home, school, or any institution produce what we consider to be undesirable results. An example of this is easily seen in a school that I am familiar with: The instructors of the school felt it was time to paddle a student when they violated certain rules. Although I personally don't believe in paddling, they felt this was their just right. There were several instructors who, for religious or medical reasons, did not paddle. They gave their reasons for not spanking, which was also their right. So here you have two different viewpoints: one set of teachers' view was that physical discipline is appropriate in school and the other view was comprised of teachers that could not or would not spank. The persons who stated their reasons against spanking were threatened with death notes in their mail boxes, along with their tires being flattened. When the standardized test was given concerning the subject of Civics, the students of the school scored way down below where they should have. This was to be expected. When the majority of a school behaves in an uncivil way, the students reflect the behavior on tests, thus showing the instructors were really good at teaching … incivility.

When we consider how to communicate in a civil manner, there are many examples we can use to show how we lack civility. A fine example is the word "evolution." This word, when used by rude, uncivil persons in the Christian community, can cause great strife. There should be made an effort to reason with each other, although we can hold different positions. We should not resort to strife in our disagreements, but rather we should see if this viewpoint is worth alienating others from us. Some tenets that we hold are non-negotiable, in light of Biblical teaching, but others are just so much "trash" as Paul would tell us.

The word "evolution", if it belongs to anyone, belongs to the Christian. It is our word. The Book tells us that it is our school master that brings us to Christ. Anytime we talk about schooling, we concern ourselves with the evolution of knowledge that has occurred over the course of time. The Book indicates that as far as mankind is concerned, God did not drop the whole load of knowledge on Adam. Instead, Man had to keep records on what he had learned, and devise strategies for retaining that which was learned in his memory. Over a period of time, the accumulated concepts of what God intends for us to know came to our generation. Therefore, our generation should be the most prolific in bringing a great host of people to the master. Instead, we enjoy bickering over differences in beliefs while a world lies dying at our door steps. We hoard the truth by concerning ourselves with how exclusive we can be. WE concern ourselves about how right we are and we talk about how wrong other Christians are.

We are attempting to show what sloppy thinkers and communicators we seem to be. We must strive to be precise, and concise, in our efforts to win a world that needs clarity. We are the ones that have the prescriptions, and we should be as careful, as the druggist in our community, to prescribe the cure. You may ask, "Do I believe in evolutionism?" No, I do not. I don't believe in any "ism" whatever. The Good Book tells us that no person can serve two masters. If he does, he will love the one and hate the other. Any person that believes in two "isms" will find himself in conflict with himself and the world he loves. His love of some his "isms" will surely banish him in exile to some remote corner of life. The person with such beliefs will deny that he loves one master more than the other through a rationalization process in his mind. But the scars from this mental conflict will always result in a lack of civility to others, especially when he is challenged on his holding of two opposing beliefs.

For me, I try to separate facts, or what can be ascertainable by our senses, and what I know by faith. I believe in God the Father, Jesus Christ, and the blessed Holy Spirit. I believe that Jesus was born of a virgin, lived as a man for a brief length of time, died on the cross, was raised on the third day, and ascended into Heaven. I believe that He lives to make intercession for us, and that there are groanings that are made in such depths they cannot be uttered. So intense is the great love that He manifests toward us. I know some things well and some things poorly, but I believe in God and his message and I don't believe in much else.

I know people who believe the world was created in six 24-hour-days, and they are wonderful Christians. Some believe that the day that is talked about represents epochs or thousands of years, and they are fine, too. Some believe in the evolution process, not evolutionism, and they are fine too. For me, if we find hard evidence for one or the other belief, that's fine too. When the island of Japan moved 15 feet east in about 10 or 15 minutes, one cannot help wondering what a twenty-four hour earthquake of that magnitude would do. If we could extrapolate the distance the crust moved during the 10 minutes to a 24 hour time frame, and add a few thousand asteroids thrown in at strategic points around the globe, we might discover quite a difference in the landscape. Maybe the earth would look a lot different. Couldn't happen in a million years, you say. Yeah, sure.

When we come to our final place with God, all the things and ideas we believe in, that lay outside the providence of God will not be worth all the strife we have caused. Winston Churchill's last words as he lay on his death bed, "I am bored with it all." We, too, will be bored with all the phony beliefs. I BELIEVE IN JESUS CHRIST AND I KNOW ABOUT OTHER THINGS.

The last example of shoddy reasoning is abortion. We know that human beings begin with a single cell in a saline solution. The cell goes through haploid and diploid cell division and growth. As time progresses, a single chamber heart comes into being, then a two chamber heart like a reptile, then a three chambered heart like birds, until the four chambered heart exists. Finally, a human being emerges into the world, and timing is everything. It does not take eons of time, rather the miracle of creating a human being occurs in about nine months. Since a woman creates a human being in a short period of time, she is like a god. This makes the person who believes there are no gods look a little foolish.

Some scientists, working in isolation somewhere in the world, are working with inanimate objects and solutions. If they create a cell in a test tube that goes through a tiny small period of cell division, he will proclaim that he has created life. All the scientists of the world, if they can duplicate the process ever so briefly, will write papers and will be held in the highest acclaim. Thus, the scientists of the world admit that life begins with a single cell. Life in the womb begins with a single cell, and when that cell is destroyed through some deliberate process, life is destroyed. The pathos of ignorance that seems to prevail when hundreds of millions of dollars and endless hours of research by our finest scientific minds goes towards trying to create life, even for a brief moment in a single cell, while at the same time destroying the work of a single cell in the womb, is at best an exercise in futility.

End of story. Case closed.

Finally, abortion leads to a problem that is hard to resolve. A baby not born today will, thirty years from now, not be in the market place buying goods and services. It is no wonder that our great cities are becoming ghost cities full of pathos and squalor since created minds capable of solving problems and creating markets will not be there. Any solution we devise to solve the job situation is only temporary.

Jobs depend on markets, and for people to participate in those markets, they must be present.

This is plausible reasoning with civility, folks; plausible reasoning.

Lesson Seven - Looking into the matter of sin

When we look into the matter of sin, we find that sin is of concern only to those who are concerned about it. As simple as this concept is, the problem is that we don't know for sure who is concerned. We do know that John16:8 indicates that one task of the Holy Spirit is to convict the world of sin. I won't get into the fact that the world itself is an inanimate object, and that Jesus is obviously talking about the world as it consists of people.

From this, we then feel assured that conviction is taking place in large numbers, and, therefore, there is some concern about integrity in dealing with the matter. Conviction, as we understand it, causes all kinds of reactions in the human emotions. Unfortunately, there are persons who, by using incorrect thinking, are able to provide false hope through the faulty advice they disperse. They do not provide answers, and the only people they really help are themselves. This type of wrong behavior is treated with reproach in the Good Book.

In the fifty years that I have spent observing the human condition, I have found that the number one cause of sin, wrong doing, or whatever you wish to call it, is a lack of self-respect. I cannot think of a single act of wrong, against the neighbor, which cannot be traced back to a lack of self-respect.

When we look at our fellow humans, we see inconsistent behaviors, and this can cause us some problems when we attempt to help them. We don't know if the person's miserable behavior is causing his emotional stress as a result of conviction, or whether he is raising hell just because he enjoys it. What we need is some kind of discernment before we act.

Certainly, if prayer is real, we need to resort to that method. When dealing with our troubled humanity, we need to forget how brilliant we think we are. We need to call on all of the resources available to us: Good pastors, Good councilors, Good priests, Good teachers, and a host of sources to deal with the problems. It was said of Jesus that He would not even hurt a bruised reed, and we need to try and be as gentle as He was when dealing with humanity. After all, are we not all hollow bruised reeds in some part? Is there not some part of us that is weak and crushed a little, thus causing us to bend to the wrong things at the wrong times? Like Jesus, we should not harm the bruised reeds around us, but let us have that something in us that will allow healing to take place. When we interact with those around us, let us be gentle as our Savior is.

There is another piece to the puzzle when we consider the consequences of sin. These are the laws that govern our communities. A person can cause an offense against his concept of God, and at the same time cause an offense against his community or culture. In terms of what we are thinking about, a person can sin against his God, and not sin against the laws of his community. Also, the same person could sin against his community and not against his God, or both things could even happen at once. As an example, suppose a person has slain another person, is brought before the bar of justice, and is convicted. While he is sitting incarcerated, he has a marvelous conversion and makes his peace with his conception of the Almighty. In spite of this, he still must face the insatiable appetite of revenge that the community has ordered. So, in dealing with shame and guilt, it is difficult to supply solutions when we don't really know the source of the shame and guilt that a particular person may have.

The final problem with reasoning with one another is the problem of language. It is almost impossible to communicate well. If you have a very clear idea, no matter how clear it is in your mind, it is almost impossible to reconstruct that same idea in another person's mind. A good example, suppose one of us speaks Spanish and cannot understand a word of English, the other one only speaks English and cannot understand Spanish. When we attempt to communicate an idea of relative importance, it seems to be an insurmountable task. As the two of us get to know one another, it becomes easier and easier to get the proposed idea across. But even if you have the same parents and are raised in the same household, it stills remains a daunting task. In my case, having nine other siblings, it seemed the most common thread said was, "I don't understand the person. What in the world is he talking about?"

With that in mind we will attempt to present the following concepts on sin. There are many ideas to consider:

One: What is sin?

Two: What is the definition of sin?

Three: What is the process of sin, or how does it happen?

Four: What is the cure for sin?

What sin is, in particular, is that which separates us from peace with the Divine. This is the simplest definition. Sin is going on right now, at this very moment. Sin is that which is not confessed, and also not attempting to set things right with our Creator. Jesus says there are two commandments that we should obey: we are to love the Lord our God with every essence of our being, and the second is to do nothing that will harm another person. We don't even want to bruise the person. Jesus said in these two statements, are found all of the Law. This is simple to state, simple to talk about, but difficult to perform.

James 2:8 tells us to love our neighbors the same way we love ourselves. What a scorcher that is. All over the world, people are obeying a distorted version of this commandment, and they feel good about it. They say, "I don't like myself, in fact I hate myself. And by following the commandment right, my neighbor better watch out, because I don't intend to treat him any better than I treat myself."

This lesson does not seem to be taught in today's Christian teaching. The commandment is clearly intended for people who have a good healthy respect for themselves. Example, I like myself and I buy myself a fine coat. In fact, I will buy two: one for myself and I will treat my neighbor, who does not have one, to a coat. I will get for myself a fine education, and I will help my neighbor receive one too. I have a nice place to sleep, and, I will help my neighbor sleep well too, where possible. On and on without end the message goes on, until all our brothers are well fed, well clothed, and well educated. Tough isn't it.

Yes, it is a tough nut to crack. How can we be charitable to others in a way that honors God? It is a conundrum; a puzzle that is difficult to solve. We, as children of God, wish to give of our time, money, and self to others. We acquire a desire to be generous by our rebirth, but the odd thing about receiving something that is free, is that quite often we don't appreciate it because it cost us nothing. Since there was no expense to us, we often misuse or abuse what others may have sacrificed to give us. Many of us have sacrificed to give to others. In fact, some people would have us go to the extreme. They think that running around in sackcloth and living on stale crackers and stagnant water in order to give others the majority of the fruits of their labors proves the superiority of their faith. I believe that is not the wisest way to be charitable. There are some clues on wise giving in the parable of the talents, and in what is commonly referred to as the "Love Chapter", I Corinthians 13. The first clue is I Timothy 5:8, and according to that verse, we need to be providing for our family first before any other obligation. The second clue is 1 Corinthians 13:3, which states that if you give all of your possessions to the poor, it doesn't benefit either the giver or the recipient unless you do it with love. So, any giving we do must be done out of love, not out of duty or because someone says you ought to. The only basis for giving should be love. The last clue is the story of the talents, where each servant was given talents according to their ability. The first 2 servants invested their money wisely, and were rewarded accordingly by their master. The third servant hoarded his money and did not even earn interest, which angered the master. This parable can be interpreted in many ways, but surely one of the obvious meanings is that to be wise in the investment of our money is a good thing. There are many other passages in The Good Book that speak of money, and our attitude toward it. But, these illustrate the view that our giving cannot be done without love, and without our investing it in some way.

Well, that pretty well sums up sin, and now to the process. We will turn to James 1:3-15. In particular, where he says that no man should say when he is tempted, that God is tempting him. Talk about using God's name in vain. I have heard all too often, "God is testing me." Whoa, we are thankful that lightening does not burn us right at that moment. James goes on to say that God cannot be tempted with sin, and neither will He tempt ANY man. You have to stop accusing others for your willful disobedience. God made the flesh; He calls it the temple of the soul. We are further told that so precious is the flesh, that whoever destroys the flesh, He will also destroy. That's found in 1 Corinthians.3:16-17; strong stuff, pretty explicit, and very clear. To him that understands, nothing more needs to be said. To him that does not understand, any explanation is possible.

So, you have to stop blaming you parents, your environment, or any other thing you want to accuse for your own willful choices. We are taught by learned professors who deal with the processes of the mind, that for a short time when we are young, we can lay blame on others. By the time a person reaches a certain age, whatever that age of accountability may be for him, he has only himself to blame since there is plenty of information available to him to help get over any handicaps. Besides, a just God will not hold a person accountable for things that are not in the person's providence to correct.

The process of sin starts with the idea of wanting something, but it is not yet lust at this initial stage. How can you tell when your wants turn into lusts? It's simple, when you want something so badly you begin to scheme about how to get it. In the scheming, lust is born. This scheming begins to drag us into the vortex of its current. When we set up schemes of lying, stealing, or defaming someone else to get what we want, or just as in the garden where the first sin was connected to deceit, then we have sin being conceived. Conception takes place right there as our lusts become inflamed. The insertion into the body of thought of the single celled embryo of scheming is the moment of conception. Believe it or not, we are still safe at this point. We can put on the brakes. When we begin to carry out our schemes, then we have the birthing of sin. Anything born of man will die somewhere, somehow, someplace. It will either be the death of a relationship, or a separation from one of the things we love. Pretty succinct description of the process, don't you think?

Now, we venture on to the cure. To detail the cure, we go to the book of Hebrews, which happens to be my favorite book in the Bible. Now, I know one should not have favorites, but I never claimed to be perfect. I am willing to discuss the Gospel with anyone, but I have a habit of no in-depth discussion unless a certain parameter is met. I have told several persons, who have attempted to draw me out, that I would like for them to sit and read the book of Hebrews at least six times. Read it like a book, sitting somewhere quiet, and read it all the way through. Read until the warp and the weave and the pattern of the fabric becomes a great tapestry, suitable to hang on the walls of your mind for private viewing from time to time.

I do not believe for a second that Paul wrote the book of Hebrews. The book does not reflect his thinking at all. Paul had changed from the hardnosed, no-holds barred persecutor of the church, into a softer man, the great ambassador of Jesus Christ. The changed Paul was willing to compromise, and rightly so when you look at his purpose. Now, this is as I see it, and I mean as I see it. I am willing to admit that sometimes I don't see things as accurately as I should, but as we say in Calculus, I am in the neighborhood. Paul was a missionary and a church builder, and when he wanted to build a church in a particular culture, he didn't hesitate to give a little. We see his willingness to compromise in Philippians 1:12-19. His goal couldn't be clearer: preach Christ. If a particular culture did not want women to speak in public meetings, so be it, but always keep in mind that in Christ, there is neither male nor female.

So, here we have an example of how we should act. If the church you are in treats the ladies as second class citizens, follow Paul's example and find a church that believes in Jesus Christ, the new birth, and has a culture you agree with. Don't fuss with the persons whose culture is different than yours. Find another church, or create one yourself. Everyone else is doing it. Now, I John 3:2-3 makes a truly remarkable statement: whatever errors we have will be washed away when we see Him as He is. We can strive to be as good as we can. We can make every effort, but in the long run, when we see Him, whatever disagreements we have will amount to nothing. Scott Adams, in his comic strip "Dilbert", makes a great statement. The Boss tells Dilbert that he does not agree with him. Dilbert responds, "Actually you don't disagree with me. No, you think you disagree with me, but you are mistaken. You're simply experiencing an illusion caused by the limits of your comprehension. If you were able to fully comprehend both the problem and my recommended solution, you would agree with me." Ain't it the truth? We need input coupled with good reasoning ability.

I don't like to argue with individuals who don't have all the information they need for good reasoning. My practice is to cause as little stress as necessary. Don't add your offense to the offense of the cross. I am not saying sins of one type are different from sins of another type, they are just different. There are different sins that Christ paid for on the cross. Again, I am not saying sins of one type are different from sins of another type, they are just different.

I cannot here go through all of the wonderful revelations to us in Hebrews. I only say if you immerse yourself in it you will find some shocking jolts to your knowledge of the message of the Gospel.

We must go on to another story here to illustrate. In old Israel, before the birth of Jesus, there lived a fine married couple by the name of John and Mary. They were outstanding people, leaders of their community, always on time for community doings, and strict observers of the Law, they were beyond reproach.

John and Mary were studious folks, and were considered by no other experts but themselves to be the best animal husbandry people around. There was no one who could hold forth on the subject with greater wisdom than themselves. John and Mary had a little discussion on the matter, and they felt that people in neighboring communities were not up-to-date on their ideas. They didn't fully appreciate John and Mary's knowledge. At the local fair, these two so-called experts had not won first prize for any of the sheep they had shown, and this was a matter of concern. One day, John said to Mary, "I have spotted the perfect ram over in a farm near the town of One-upmanship, and I think we can negotiate for the prize ram." Mary said, "Go for it, for we are standing still with our current flock, and everyone knows that no matter how smart you are, you have to have fine talent."

John then travels over near One-upmanship and negotiates for the ram. After some talk, an agreement was made, a handshake was done, and John was indentured. Time passed, and John received the ram and brought it Home. They were both excited and tapped the keg (back then they were allowed), brought all their neighbors in, and threw a party. John then stated that over in Podunk he had spotted the perfect ewe, and he thought they should buy that as well. Again Mary said, "Yes, let's do it." John again negotiated, shook hands, and brought home the ewe. This time, they did not celebrate as hard as before.

They felt a little guilty about how rambunctious they had partied during the last celebration.

Time passed, and the ewe brought forth her first ram, and what a magnificent animal it was. But, there was a problem that kept raising its ugly head. John felt guilty, because although no one else knew it, he had slacked off as he worked for the ram and the ewe. He hadn't done his best while working for the other farmers. John talks to Mary about the guilt problem, and she felt a little guilty too. Together they agreed to take the prize ram to the temple to be sacrificed in order to get rid of their guilt. They were well aware that their neighbors were watching, and would treat them with high respect for their devotion to the law. At least, they felt some benefit should be coming from the act of contrition, but on the way home they discussed the affair and admitted that they still felt guilty. The next year, they do the same and still they felt guilty. There was a reason and Hebrews 10:1-18 handles the problem very well. For the blood of the sacrificed animal could not take away guilt, therefore they continued to make the trip year after year.

Hebrews 10 says this man, Jesus, in one act took away the guilt that resulted from Adam's sin, the sin nature we have inherited. God states that in the new birth, he installs a new heart of flesh which may not always be successful as we would like, but has the possibility to be. And with this heart comes the will to do what the Father wants, without our being concerned with either reward or punishment. And I am certainly willing, although I still deal with what I want. Paul says he was all right until he ran across the tenth commandment. He said that it had a tendency to slay him, and it does me as well.

This act by Jesus raises another problem which persons who say they believe find hard to deal with. If the guilt is taken care of by His efforts, and it is as effective as He says it is, why are we telling our children to let your conscience be your guide? The conscience feeds off of our feelings of guilt and shame, but our guilt and shame are covered over by the cross. This leaves us with the conclusion that the conscience is defective and untrustworthy when it prompts those feelings in us. For my part, I never felt much guilt before I was committed to Christ, and I certainly do not feel a lot of guilt now. I just don't have many regrets, which shows to me at least that I had better come up with another system, and I have. I do not trust my conscience.

The system I use to guide my life is simple, but it does have some difficulties. The system has at its core Colossians 3:16: Let the word of Christ dwell in you richly. There is the word "let" again. The second part of the system is found in Psalms 119 where it says: Thy word have I hid in my heart, that I might not sin against thee. This is pure and simple in its beauty, but difficult to do in daily living. When I saw these words, I decided to install the great prism in my mind with everything having to be refocused through it. I tried to make the Word the plumb bob for my life. I started this in 1962, and while I have had more than my share of failures, the happiness and joy that have resulted in mine and my wife's life has reaped a cup indeed running over. We both resolved to do this at the same time. It took time to make the system more effective, but we are more than satisfied with the work we have put into the system.

Of course, this takes care of one group of sins, but to take care of the ongoing day by day sins of daily living requires us to do something else. These are the sins of the will, where we sin either by commission or omission. These sins are taken care of completely by 1 John 1:9. If we confess our sins, He is faithful and just to forgive us of our sins, and to cleanse us from ALL unrighteousness. This is marvelous. The Christian who enters the continuing process of owning their sin is cleaned, and the record in the book of life shows a clean slate. Now, this feeds into Paul's admonition to pray without ceasing, always keeping oneself in the position of acknowledging our own wrongdoing. If a person is that serious about wrongdoing and has to acknowledge it, he becomes careful about what he does. The beauty of owning and confessing your own sins is that even if you are not a professing Christian, you know the system works. The person who covers his sin, and does not own up to them, is in large trouble if the wrong doing is found out later on. When the truth is concealed and is later revealed, sometimes more damage will be done by the cover-up than the deed itself.

Lesson Eight - "Not sin"

I know there are devotees of the different authors throughout the world, and one of them may read this book by some intervention of life and recognize an idea from their favorite author. To be honest, I have read a lot of books, and if you see some idea that has sprung from one of your favorites, then that is good. This means that my reading was not in vain, and perhaps I had understood better than I have dreamed of.

There is one author in particular I must mention here; Pierre Teilhard de Chardin, 1881-1955. He was an outstanding mystic, Catholic Priest, and an anthropologist. I read an interpretation of his book in the early 1960's, and was enthralled by it. The book was terrific. At the time, I was engaged in a profession where two of my immediate supervisors were of the Catholic belief. They appeared to be very faithful in following the tenets of their religion, so I took the book to them. I told them I was mystified by it, and they said, "Weaver, there you go again. You need to relax. The Pope has said he does not understand the writings either."

Since then, I have read everything that I could get my hands on by Chardin, and have most, if not all, of the interpretations of his writings. My view of the man is he was caught between two religions. He was an ardent evolutionist believing in the religion of evolutionism. He also skirted or toyed with some form of pantheism. Though, there could be no mistake that he was a stout, no-holds-barred person of integrity, along with being a fervent lover of Jesus Christ. In my opinion, there is no doubt about that. He spent his life attempting to place them together into a new religion. Of course, this is my take of the person, right or wrong, but we need to get to the core of where, in my view, he excelled. He lived in exile, because his views differed from the thoughts of the Catholic Authorities. As a result, he labored in the most poverty stricken places of the world. In doing so, he came up with these observations as I envision them. Since I cannot read French, I have to put up with interpretations of his works, so hopefully he may not mind if I interpret his ideas. Besides, where he is, his errors have been corrected just as ours will be. In his labors in remote parts of the world, he observed that persons raised in the most miserable conditions were able to rise to great heights by dent of their spirits and efforts. He also noticed that persons raised in sumptuous conditions often sank to great depths of degradation. From this, he projected the observation that environment and parenting skills had little to nothing to do with future success.

To illustrate further, let us pretend in some miserable place in the world a soul is born. The soul reaches a certain level of thought, becomes aware somehow there is a divine power, and makes every effort at its disposal to become closer to that's soul's level of perception of the divine. The Father above may say "That soul has done well in that environment, and so is a good candidate for a perfect environment with me. For if he desires to improve that much, he will flourish here." Let's say another soul is born into a perfect environment, as is defined by his fellow beings. He is taught the best of manners, completely enjoys his culture, and is regarded as a superb being. However, he is not interested in the divine and makes no effort in that direction. Instead, he writes pamphlets detailing how foolish believers are. The Father above observing this may say, "This one is not a good candidate for my perfect environment."

Teilhard seems to say that one man sees a mountain and curses it, while another man sees the mountain and can't wait to interrupt his daily work to travel great distances, at great expense, to play on the mountain. One man is thrown into a body of water, and through fear and much flailing of his extremities, he manages to escape and curses the water. Another man, with the same experience, is filled with great joy and can't wait to be thrown in again. Obviously, it is not the environment at fault. Each person must use the leverage of his mind and body parts, apply his efforts against the obstacles, and rise to greater levels of growth. Instead of viewing the environment as evil, we can view it as the very help to our future growth.

We then must see that sin is vanquished in our lives when we do something with the right mind and intent. We can't talk about sin without spending some time on "not sin", or what isn't sin in our daily lives. The scripture talks about whatever we do in word or deed, whether we eat or drink, we should do to the glory of Jesus Christ. In these words are found the essence of what is "not sin." These words brings us to what may or not be the wrong with the way we look at what we hate or love. The statements that we are to hate certain things of the world can lead to some misunderstanding. It is the same with the word "world" or any other word. To clear things up, we turn to Amos 5:15 where we are admonished to hate the evil but love the good. If this is so, we need a fine understanding of what is good and what is evil. This is very clear; anything that detracts us from our love of God or harms our neighbor is evil, and anything that nourishes us toward a deeper love of Christ and neighbor is good. We need to be careful how we treat those things that exist for Him. This is the premise for what I say here in this section. The soul exists for God. As a matter of fact, every piece of matter exists for God, this includes the whole universe.

"Not sin" revolves around a simple concept: whatever we do, we must do to glorify God. This of course brings us farther along. The substances, the goods, the services, and the water that nourished the babe Jesus and caused him to grow from babe to full fruition as a man has to be considered good, maybe even divine. The persons that produced those goods and services that nourished him were "not sin", and so can be considered good if they did it with the intent of helping their neighbor as a tribute to God. If our souls exist for the glory of God, anything that nourishes that soul and causes the soul to grow and expand in its work of Glorying God is good. If there are things in this world that enhances our drive toward Jesus Christ, then those things cannot be bad, and how can we hate the things that nourishes us and our neighbor.

Any person that desires to make an opus of his life, out of necessity, must use the ingredients of the world: the people, the buildings, and the things of our environment. Anything that gives us an opportunity to allow the presence of Christ to shine in our lives must be treated with respect, and we must be a good steward of those things. The purpose of the environment that God placed us in was to take us from being a small baby and grow us into the age of accountability, while giving us the opportunity to enlarge our souls and bring all our fruits of our labor, nourished by God's efforts, to the feet of Christ our Lord.

We commune with Christ through our activities toward our neighbor who is in the world and of His creation. When we commune with Christ through our God-intended efforts, we fulfill the highest calling for which man is created. Each act, then, is like a molecule of water. When added to the tiny acts of another Christ-inspired individual, and then another, and still another, it then becomes a mighty stream of actions that creates a current, drawing the unsaved into the knowledge of Christ through us. If we don't act correctly, the work does not get done. When we act correctly, the work gets done. So, by Christ's work in us, it is what we do in spirit that becomes a mighty current of divinity.

We sometimes look at our daily work: catching the bus, driving a truck, building something, whatever we are doing, as not being in touch with God. We fail to see that God does His work, and to Him, His work may be commonplace, just as our work too often feels commonplace to us. When we look at our daily routine properly, we see that what we do provides substance for others, food, clothing, shelter and the material needs of life. That, unknown to us, some small babe may receive our efforts, and is able to grow into full adulthood. Perhaps they cure some disease, or at least feed into the process of benefiting others. It is all the same, whether a small deed or a large deed. Our daily work is not subtracted from glorifying Christ, but if done properly, increases our moments with Him. We do not steal time from Him by living an ordinary life that is full of service for others.

The secret of the divine is to daily practice the seeking out of the reflection of His image in our fellow beings. We must see that whatever we do in word or deed is done simply to the glory of God. Sitting and doing nothing brings a stupor onto our souls and spirits. In other words, we become tepid, neither hot nor cold. This is a state that we have been warned to avoid.

Final Words

It is impossible to understand the great success that Christ has done. I am not the least surprised by the success of Joel Osteen. Here is a person who admits to bypassing the learned theologians of seminary prestige. He has scratched the surface of the success of Jesus the Christ, and, as a result, is drawing many to his ministry. He is criticized for the lack of scripture reference, but the truth of the matter is simple: truth is truth, with or without reference.

In the 1950's when I was young and ardently pursuing the ministry, we preachers had an outstanding thought about seminary. When we got together and would speak about seminary, we used to call it "cemetery." We would observe some young pastor who was very successful being told to get more education. The young pastor would go away to seminary and never be heard of again. His fire and zeal had somehow faded away. A successful young pastor going on for more education, and then not having any zeal, would end up teaching in a Bible college. Perhaps Osteen needs to go to seminary. I AM NOT AGAINST EDUCATION, I AM AGAINST PEOPLE WHO THINK THEY HAVE ARRIVED!

All across the world, there are an untold number of good and fine persons. If we understand the process, anyone who is devoted to the route of confession and setting things correct, where possible, is at that moment cleanse of all their unrighteousness and no sin is recorded in the Book of Life. In other words, that person is a saint and a priest to his God. The success of Christ is beyond our understanding. Just as a house divided against itself finds it just a struggle to survive, so does the divided Christian mind find itself in a death-defying struggle to live. The struggle is like a person thrashing in a flood; they are flinging their arms about to try to keep their head above water. They are not happy with their existence because they have no peace, no contentment. Until they decide which master they will serve, the struggle will continue for them.

We have to have confidence in the mind of Christ that He is able to fully do what He has set out to do. Our minds cannot be divided if we are to survive as a human being that is fully developed and mature. We can begin our path to a mature life by making an offering of our wills to Christ. The offering that we bring at the end of our stay on earth is to be a fully developed person worthy of the price Christ has paid. We have to question our thought life to see if we measure up to the mind of Christ. The thought that I am interested in is simple, do I love a particular culture more than I love Christ?

I was born, as I said, in 1931, and what a time it was. From 1931 to 1941, a dynamic change was occurring around me. The horse drawn buggy was dying yet still trying to compete with an automobile. The horse and plow were competing with the tractor. The iceman would come once a week and chip a twenty five pound block of ice, or perhaps a fifty pound block as finances would dictate. He would, with a grin, hoist the block on his shoulders fully aware that we children were scrambling for little chips of ice. What a grand time it was, but that culture was fading fast. Still there were people that felt the closeness of their Christ and were successful in Him.

In 1941 through 1950, dramatic changes were challenging the believer. Hitler, Japan, war, rationing, and a host of really difficult life changing cultural elements were everywhere present. Still, the true believer soldiered on confident in the future and their Christ.

In the early fifties and sixties, the culture solidified and I was fully dedicated to it. The barber cut my hair every Saturday night to perfection. On Sunday, I put on my double breasted suit with a white shirt and tie, cufflinks, and tie tack. My wing-tip shoes were polished and shining. I went to church somber and reflective. I had arrived, and I was right in all things, not to be questioned. Then it happened: Woodstock, Vietnam, girls with no bras, Kent state, and a whole flood of new issues came crashing on my mind. A great unsettling took place in my thinking, but still Christ was more than sufficient for the time.

From 1965 until now, more and more changes are taking place. We need to stop with our negative attitudes of loving the past culture more than we love our Christ. The old ways are gone forever and we cannot bring them back, nor should we want to. I watch auctions taking place where they bid on an abandoned storage room. I watch participants bidding on a bin that is full of several generations of accumulated possession. It is these objects that once were sacred artifacts which someone packed away with great care. This was the history of a family; this was their treasured past. I watch the winner dive in, rifling through the stacks of containers, throwing boxes on the floor. He is looking for the one or two items that may bring him some profit, but to him the rest is junk, garbage. We should be telling the future generations that as Christ has met us in the past, He is more than able to do so in the future. Like the old missionary once said, "The future is as bright as the promises of God." The past is meaningless, let us look toward that bright future.

I realize the biggest change is in front of us. Romans 1:1-20 talks about learning from our environment. The great tree in the forest, living in the prime spot, gathers the resources of nature and becomes a mighty big tree. The trees form their seeds in the spring, which fall to the ground and germinate. The seedlings fail to grow because the mature trees have tied up the resources available for growth. We must relinquish the prominent favorite place in society, and yield to the growth of future generations, being sure to sell them on the idea that Christ will meet their needs. We must be willing to give up some of our stored resources for the benefit of those coming after us, or God will do it for us.

The story can be best told by the following example. Years ago I wrote this short story and only my wife was aware of its existence. I did nothing further with this story, but will use it to illustrate how we should be enthusiastic for God's love. A father and mother were working very hard, and at the end of the day went by the day care and picked up their son. They were worried and greatly concerned. They had studied hard and had gone through all the motions that were supposed to guarantee success. Both were aware that they were not prepared for the changes ahead, realizing that their care and training had not equipped them for a changing work place.

When they arrived at home, they were so engrossed in their concerns for work that they did not notice, as they should, the desires of the little boy. The father had settled himself in his chair and was easing his burden by watching the news. The little boy tugged at his father's trousers and with great insistence said, "Daddy play with me." The father wanting peace, reached into his pocket and took out a dollar. He said, "Here, go buy yourself some ice cream at the corner store," and off the little fellow went perfectly happy with the gift. In another case with the same scene, another little boy came and asked the father to play with him. Again, we see the father trying to give the boy a gift. The boy, with tears in his eyes, tells his father, "I don't want the gift. I want your presence in my life."

Here is the difference that we might, in our humanity, exhibit to our Heavenly Father. We are not enamored with the gifts or opportunities that come from the Father. Great as those things are, we want on a daily basis fellowship with the person who said, "I am with you always."

There are coral reefs in the bottom of the cold inhospitable sea. They cannot be seen clearly because of the inadequate light that penetrates from the surface. When a diver puts on a special apparatus of underwater lights, he can penetrate the darkness of the ocean depth and see such beauty that often he is stunned. I believe that each soul is a thing of great beauty, and each person is given by God a soul of incredible beauty. It is what the person does with his soul that either can enhance or shatter the beauty. If we could put on our special diving apparatus and dive into the sea of humanity, using the light that emanates from God, we would see the beauty of the souls that God sees. Unfortunately we cannot do this, but we can allow the light of God's love to illuminate the lives around us.

Conclusion

I would like to end on a lighter note. I believe I too was given a beautiful soul. In my case, it was a 1941 robin egg blue Ford convertible with a flat head V8 motor. I believe I took that soul, drove it horribly, and altered it. I played with the engine, moved the timing just a shade forward, and altered the looks unthinkingly to my liking. I drove it through all kinds of terrible mischief until it was a mess.

I heard in Psalm 23 about a master restorer, and I went to Him with my problem. He took that soul and refurbished it to mint factory condition. He handed me a manual for the soul, and said cruise carefully, follow the manual, and I will keep the soul in top running condition.

If, while cruising around, you come across a soul that is a 1941 robin egg blue Ford convertible with a flat head engine, I will be delighted. Perhaps, we will stop and park, and talk about how we need to keep bitterness, anger, hate, and other distasteful ingredients out of the oil. The acid from such harmful components eats at the bearings and makes the soul run erratic. We will talk about keeping the brakes in tip top condition, for in cruising we can sometimes run into situations that could damage the car or engine if we don't slow down or stop. Perhaps, we will run into others just like us, and we will gather some morning in a meeting. The Master Restorer will be there, for He has said where any of you gather there I am going to be.

Perhaps, He will say, "Enough of parking and talking, you should be out cruising. There are other souls that need restored, and when they see the fine job I have done with you, perhaps they will bring their souls to me". So ladies and gentlemen, start your engines.

I bid you adieu.

About the Author

Ralph Weaver has worked at many occupations in his life, but none more so important than father. He and his wife, Hannah, sacrificed much for their children. I ought to know, they are my parents. Recently my dad was diagnosed with Alzheimer's and part of his personal fight against this disorder has been to write. His writing has included some of the wisdom he has shared with me, my sister, brother, his grandchildren and those young persons that have come into his life through teaching that he considers his "adopted" children. I consider these writings as part of our inheritance.